FINDING A CHURCH YOU CAN LOVE

AND LOVING *the* CHURCH YOU'VE FOUND

FINDING
A CHURCH
YOU CAN LOVE

AND LOVING
the CHURCH
YOU'VE FOUND

KEVIN & SHERRY HARNEY

ZONDERVAN

GRAND RAPIDS, MICHIGAN 49530 USA

We want to hear from you. Please send your comments about this book to us in care of zreview@zondervan.com. Thank you.

ZONDERVAN™

Finding a Church You Can Love and Loving the Church You've Found
Copyright © 2003 by Kevin and Sherry Harney

Requests for information should be addressed to:

Zondervan, *Grand Rapids, Michigan 49530*

Library of Congress Cataloging-in-Publication Data

Harney, Kevin.
    Finding a church you can love and loving the church you've found /
Kevin and Sherry Harney.
      p. cm.
    ISBN 0-310-24679-2
    1. Choice of church.   I. Harney, Sherry, 1960–   II. Title.
BV640.H37 2003
250—dc21
                                           2003011916

Published in association with the literary agency of Ann Spangler and Company, 1420 Pontiac Road S.E., Grand Rapids, MI 49506.

Interior design by Beth Shagene

Printed in the United States of America

---

03 04 05 06 07 08 09 /❖ DC/ 10 9 8 7 6 5 4 3 2 1

To Jesus Christ,
the great Bridegroom,
who loves his church (his people)
with an everlasting love.

Also to the church of Jesus Christ
all over the world, his beloved bride.
You are his plan to bring divine love
to a broken world.

Contents

Preface

THIS BOOK WAS DESIGNED TO BE USER FRIENDLY. It is a tool to help you through the process of finding a church you can really love. We have done a few things to make this resource helpful and easy to use.

We have kept the chapters short. We have tried to keep each chapter as brief as possible, while still covering the most important information. Our goal is to keep your reading to a minimum so that you can devote most of your time to reflection and to taking action in finding a church you can love and loving the church you have found.

We have sought to keep it practical. Being practical has been our goal each step of the way as we have written this book. You will find that each of the brief chapters ends with some kind of practical application. We have presented many ideas for personal reflection, additional study, and actions you can take in your journey of finding your way into active participation in the church, Christ's family.

We have provided opportunities for personal reflection. Each chapter has some closing questions that will help you go a little deeper into the content of the chapter. We have worded these questions so that they will be useful whether you are looking for a church as an individual, as a couple, or as a family. Individuals may use these questions for personal reflection, while couples and families can use them for discussion.

How to use this book to your advantage. There are two ways you can use this book. First, you can begin on page one and walk though the process of becoming part of a church from beginning to end, using the exercises to help you each step of the way. This approach will allow you to think through the whole process in a clear and systematic way. Or you may want to read only the chapters that connect with your felt needs and apply to where you are in your church-search journey.

This book is designed to be a tool that anyone can use, regardless of background. If you have never set foot in a church, have no religious heritage, and don't have any idea how to take the first step, this book is for you. If you have been in the church since the day you were born and have always been an active part of God's family but now feel the need to find a new church, this book will be a great help to you also.

No matter where you start, this book will serve as a road map to help you make sense of your journey as you seek to find a church you can love and to love the church you've found.

Acknowledgments

LIFE IS FILLED WITH COUNTLESS RELATIONSHIPS and connections that intertwine in ways we often fail to notice. As we look at this book, we realize how many people have helped form the materials and tools you have in your hands. We will list those we can remember and apologize in advance to those we might have forgotten.

We want to acknowledge and thank those who have been our partners in the writing and publishing of this book. Ann Spangler and Linda Peterson-Kenny had the original vision for this book and guided us through the publishing process. Jack Kuhatschek gave all the editorial support a writing team could dream to have and offered wisdom on this book that went far beyond editorial help. His knowledge of the church and love for the body of Christ helped to shape this book. We want to give special acknowledgment to the entire team at Zondervan. In over a decade of working in partnership with all of you, we have been consistently impressed with your love for God and your devotion to offering resources that will strengthen and bless the local church. You are a joy!

We also want to thank those who are part of the local churches that have shaped and formed each of us over our years of faith.

Sherry acknowledges and gives thanks to God for the people who make up: Fourth Reformed Church in Holland, Michigan; First Assembly of God (now named Grand Rapids First) in Grand Rapids, Michigan; Chino Reformed Church in Chino, California; Vineyard Christian Fellowship in Anaheim, California; New Hope Community Church in Glendora, California; Zion Reformed Church in Grandville, Michigan; and Corinth Reformed Church in Byron Center, Michigan.

Kevin acknowledges and gives thanks to God for the people who make up: Crystal Cathedral in Garden Grove, California; Vineyard Christian Fellowship in Anaheim, California; Wheaton College Church in Wheaton, Illinois; New Hope Community Church in Glendora, California; Zion Reformed Church in Grandville, Michigan; and Corinth Reformed Church in Byron Center, Michigan.

These groups of believers have been our friends and our family, and have taught us how to love and follow God in life-changing ways. We are thankful for each of them.

Introduction

Kevin's Story

My *only* memory of church from my early childhood is of an experience that ended in tragedy.

I have hazy pictures in my mind of one Sunday morning many years ago. Hard wooden benches. A cross on the wall, with a man hanging by nails driven through his hands and feet. A young boy with a crew cut and very uncomfortable clothes. The feeling that it would never end.

I remember getting out of my seat and wandering off. Like the swallows of Capistrano, I headed instinctively toward the place where I had seen punch and cookies as we had entered earlier. The surface of the counter was just above my head, but this would not stop my young hands from grasping the prize of freshly baked cookies. I had to satisfy my growling stomach, and the answer was just inches above my line of sight. I took hold of the counter's edge and began to pull myself up, certain that I was only inches from mounds of snacks and rivers of punch loaded with sugar and red dye number five.

I immediately realized something was wrong.

Instead of pulling myself up to behold the treats my taste buds longed for, I felt the entire counter began to move. It was falling toward—or more precisely, *on*—me. If this was to be the end of my young life, what better way to die than under a mountain of cookies!

I did not die. I also was not buried under a pile of cookies. My swallowlike instincts had led me to the place of cookies and punch, but I had failed to take note of one important detail: it was also the place where they had just poured many cups of scalding coffee. I remember my back hitting the floor, the counter landing on my chest, and a wave of coffee, punch, and cookies cascading over my face. I don't remember ever attending church again as a young boy.

Sherry and I come from dramatically different backgrounds. I was the bad boy, the teacher's nightmare, a non-church-attending beach bum from southern California. Sherry was a good girl, a hard-working student, a twice-a-Sunday-and-Wednesday-night church attender from a small town in western Michigan. In many ways her life experience was the opposite of mine.

Sherry's Story

For me, church and life were inextricably intertwined. Some of my fondest memories from childhood are of the days I could walk to church with my father. Church was the place where family gathered, friends played, and the teaching of the Bible helped make sense of life's toughest problems. The only trouble I would get in at church was when my whole family was sitting in the car waiting to go home and I was still inside talking with other church members. Come to think of it, there are still many Sundays when I am the last one to leave the church building.

Yet with all of my fine church training, I kept a secret hidden in my heart, a secret that I did not dare tell my family and friends. When I thought about it, I felt uncomfortable, so I remained silent for many, many years. People would laugh at me, I thought to myself. They would never understand. My secret would stay just that, a secret!

What was my hidden dream?

I wanted to marry a pastor! I so loved the church and had such deep respect for my pastor's wife that my heart's desire was to one day marry a pastor and spend my life helping people discover the joys of knowing Jesus and the satisfaction of being part of a healthy Christian church.

When Worlds Collide

Sherry and I are still very different. She always dreamed of being a pastor's wife. I never, in my wildest imagination, dreamed of being a pastor. Yet by the grace of God, we have both discovered the incredible joy of being part of the church. Sherry was born into the church family. I came as a troubled outsider who has been lovingly adopted. Both of us have learned that there are many churches we can really love and that there are many wonderful churches that will love us back.

The Big Picture

Since you are holding this book in your hands, it means one of two things has happened: You have taken the time to pick up a book whose express goal is to help you find a church you can love. Or someone who cares deeply about you has taken the time to buy this book and give it to you as a gift. However this book has ended up in your hands, we believe it is not a coincidence.

In the pages that follow, we want to offer you practical and fun tools for finding a church you can really love. We will do this by walking through the process with you. In part 1 of this book, we have attempted to present a clear picture of a healthy, biblical church. God calls the church his bride, and he loves the church as a groom loves his radiant bride. We need to see the church through his eyes.

Part 2 will help you discover how to connect with the church that is right for you. In a family, we know that people are different, and we need to learn how to get along with each other. But as you seek to find a church family, it is critical that you find the right fit.

Part 3 will help you discover how you can love the church you've found. We will also discuss how you can find your place in the church. Just as every part of a physical body has an important function, you will have an important role to play in your new church. Not only will you receive from your new church, but you will also have the joy of giving back.

Both Sherry and I believe that being part of a church can be one of the most joy-filled, life-giving experiences you will ever have. Our prayer is that you will start and end this journey knowing that as much as you would like to find a church you can love, God wants this for you even more than you do!

PART 1

UNDERSTANDING
THE CHURCH

A Radiant Bride

BRIDES ARE BEAUTIFUL. There's just no other way to put it. They are radiant, stunning, spectacular.

As a pastor, I have conducted many weddings and wedding rehearsals. The rehearsals are often informal affairs. The wedding party comes in their casual clothes. If it is a summer wedding, they might arrive in shorts and T-shirts. Let's just say that at many rehearsals, people look a little shabby . . . myself included!

But twenty-four hours later, it's a different story. This same group of people has gone through an amazing metamorphosis. Tuxedos and beautiful dresses have replaced casual clothes. And the bride has changed more than anyone!

I have the privilege of standing next to the groom as he watches his beloved bride walk down the aisle. Don't get me wrong, this same woman was beautiful the day before, but on the wedding day, there is something different about her. A glow, a spark, a radiance seems to emanate from the bride on her wedding day.

The moment the bride is about to walk down the aisle, something marvelous happens. The eyes of the groom lock onto hers. She smiles, beams, and begins walking toward him. This moment is always captured on film, but the snapshot never does justice to it. At this moment the joy and love are palpable.

The Heavenly Groom and His Church

When I think of the Bible's portrayal of the church as Jesus' bride, I always picture the moment the groom first sees his bride on their wedding day. The excitement, passion, and depth of love the groom feels is how Jesus feels about his church.

What an astonishing reality! God looks on the church with passionate love. And his church is his people. The church is you; the church is me. It is all those who believe in Jesus Christ by faith. The church is people! We are his beloved bride.

Take a moment to reflect on what the Bible says about Christ's church:

> I am jealous for you with the jealousy of God himself. For I promised you as a pure bride to one husband, Christ.
>
> —2 Corinthians 11:2 NLT

> Husbands, love your wives, just as Christ loved the church and gave himself up for her to make her holy, cleansing her by the washing with water through the word, and to present her to himself as a radiant church, without stain or wrinkle or any other blemish, but holy and blameless.
>
> —Ephesians 5:25–27

The Beloved of God

The church is not a building, an organization, or some denominational set of rules and regulations. Sometimes we get this mixed up. We say things like, "Let's go to church," as if the church is a place or a building. But in reality, the church is the people who follow Jesus. We are his bride.

Why is the image of the church as the bride of Christ so important? This image is critical for us to understand because it reveals a deep spiritual truth that often gets overlooked: God loves us! He truly does. He is passionate about us. When he looks at us, his heart skips a beat. He sees us as radiant and wonderful. God has a picture of us walking down the center aisle, and he sees us as beautiful.

It has been said that if God had a refrigerator, our picture would be on it! We matter to him. He holds us in his heart with everlasting love.

This is not to say that God forgets what we looked like on rehearsal night. It's just that he chooses to see us in the eternal present moment of the bride walking down the aisle. His heart overflows, and he exults over us with joy.

Why Be Part of the Church?

God loves his church, and we should too! Jesus calls us his bride. That one pure moment of joy and celebration on a wedding day can be yours and mine. And when we become part of his church, this rejoicing does not last for just an hour, a day, or even a lifetime; it lasts for eternity. You see, the Bible talks about a marriage supper in heaven. This same inexpressible joy will be enjoyed forever.

> Then the angel said to me, "Write: 'Blessed are those who are invited to the wedding supper of the Lamb!'" And he added, "These are the true words of God."
>
> —Revelation 19:9

We are invited to the wedding supper of Jesus. But we won't be sitting in a seat way in the back. Through faith in Jesus, we become part of his church. We are his bride. We will have the seat of honor next to Jesus. With Jesus, we will be served first when the supper begins. We will be at his side, hand in hand. When the music begins, we will get the first dance. What a beautiful picture of God's love for his people, the church!

Must I Sit in a Church Building to Be Part of the Church?

Some people will say, "I have faith in God, and I believe in Jesus, but I don't want to be part of a congregation." We have heard people say, "I don't like 'organized religion.' I will just worship on my own. I will take walks in God's creation and let that be my church experience." Many people today miss out on so much of the joy of their faith because they walk through their spiritual lives alone.

The local church is God's expression of his bride on the earth today. Do you have to sit in a church building every Sunday to be part of God's church? No! But God has established his church to bring joy to his heart and to be a blessing in our lives. The church is the place where we can discover who we really are. People all over the world are seeking to find the meaning of life and who they are. They search in bars, beds, books, on the ladder of success, and anywhere they feel there might be answers. Yet so often they end up emptier and less sure of who they are. In a healthy and biblical church, you begin to see yourself as the beloved of God. You begin to understand that you are the apple of his eye.

Look in the Mirror

What do you see when you look in the mirror? Do you see a person who is loved by God? Are you astounded that your reflection is a portrait of someone who matters more to Jesus than words could ever say? When you look in the mirror, do you ever stand in awe, knowing that God calls you his beloved? When was the last time you were overwhelmed by the fact that the Father loves you passionately? He does! You are the apple of his eye. You are his beloved. You are the romance of his heart.

If you have faith in God through Jesus Christ, you are part of his church. Each time you gather with the people of God, you see a reminder of a spiritual reality that is often forgotten. In a sense, you see a snapshot of heaven. God's people are the bride, and Jesus is the groom. Your participation in the fellowship of the church is a regular reminder of just how much God loves you!

Prayer Direction

- Pray for God to help you see yourself as his beloved bride, even on days when you don't feel all that radiant.
- Invite God to prepare your heart for the process of finding a church you can really love.

For Further Reflection

- How do you feel when you realize that Jesus sees all those who are part of his church like a radiant bride?
- If you are a Christian, what does this chapter tell you about how you should see yourself?

Action You Can Take

Bible Study

Read the following passages from the Bible:

- Psalm 136:1–5
- John 3:16–21
- Romans 8:37–39
- 1 John 4:10–11

Reflect on or discuss the following questions:

- What has God done to prove how deep his love is for you?
- If you lived each day with an absolute conviction that these passages from the Bible are true about you, how would this impact how you see yourself? How would it alter the way you see each person in the church?

Just for Fun

Picture It

If you have a picture of a bride and groom who mean a lot to you, take it out and post it where you will see it regularly. Keep it there during the whole time you are reading this book and looking for a church. Let this picture remind you that those who are truly part of Christ's church are his beloved bride. Let this also prompt you to pray for God's leading as you look for a church home.

Chapter 2

What You Believe Really Does Matter

A MOTHER WAS PREPARING A HAM for a big holiday dinner for the whole family. Before she put the ham in the pan, she cut off both ends and set them aside. Her son was watching and asked, "Mommy, why did you cut off the ends of the ham?" She said, "Well, honey, that's what my mom always did when she prepared a ham. You will have to ask Grandma when she gets here this afternoon." When Grandma arrived, the little boy asked her the same question. She gave the same answer but suggested they call her mother and investigate further. When she got the little boy's great-grandmother on the phone, he asked his question one more time. "Why did you always cut off the ends of the ham before you cooked it?" Her answer surprised him and each person he told. She said, "My pan was too small to fit the whole ham!"

Some people approach church the same way. If you ask them why they attend, they don't really know. They attend because their parents and grandparents were Catholic, Lutheran, or Baptist, and attending church is part of their family heritage. These people sometimes spend many years attending church services without ever digging deeply into their faith and what the Bible says a follower of Christ needs to believe. As a result, they never come to a personal understanding of how their beliefs should shape and guide their lives.

But the church is more than a social club, and far more than simply reciting the same words our ancestors have spoken. To understand the church, we must know what the Bible teaches and what the church believes. We should look for certain core beliefs in any church, such as the faithful preaching of God's Word, a commitment to the truth, and a call for people to truly follow Jesus. When searching for a new church home, you must know what you believe and take the time to learn what the church believes. Doctrine does matter, and the time to be sure your beliefs line up with a particular church's is *before* you join!

Why Do Core Beliefs Matter So Much?

If you are going to find a church you really love, you need to be sure that the beliefs you hold dear are part of the fabric of the congregation you are thinking of joining. If you see a certain belief as essential, and the church you are attending does not, you might find yourself experiencing inner conflict and outer tension within a short period of time.

Some beliefs should be core for all those who call themselves Christians. Although this is not a book on Christian beliefs, we should take a moment to identify the common ground on which all Christians stand. Here are some examples:

The Bible is God's Word and the authority for our beliefs and lives. This might seem obvious to most, but if you begin attending a church that seems to fit and later find out they do not hold to the authority of the Bible, you will run into all kinds of problems (2 Tim. 3:16).

Salvation comes by God's grace through faith in Jesus Christ alone. If you discover your new church does not believe that Jesus is the only way to salvation, this will quickly become a cause for you to declare "irreconcilable differences."

> For it is by grace you have been saved, through faith—and this not from yourselves, it is the gift of God—not by works, so that no one can boast.
>
> —Ephesians 2:8–9

> Jesus answered, "I am the way and the truth and the life. No one comes to the Father except through me."
>
> —John 14:6

> Salvation is found in no one else, for there is no other name [than the name of Jesus] under heaven given to men by which we must be saved.
>
> —Acts 4:12

God is Trinity. The Christian church has always affirmed that God exists in eternal Trinity. One God revealed in three persons: Father, Son, and Holy Spirit. Some congregations claim to be Christians but deny the Trinity. It is important to know a church's belief on the Trinity before moving forward too far in your relationship with them (John 14).

> Therefore go and make disciples of all nations, baptizing them in the name of the Father and of the Son and of the Holy Spirit.
>
> —Matthew 28:19

> To God's elect, . . . who have been chosen according to the fore-
> knowledge of God the Father, through the sanctifying work of the
> Spirit, for obedience to Jesus Christ and sprinkling by his blood . . .
>
> —1 Peter 1:2

Jesus Christ is divine. If a church denies that Jesus was God in human flesh, they are compromising the clear teaching of the Bible. It is critical to learn whether the church you are visiting believes Jesus is exactly who he said he is.

> In the beginning was the Word, and the Word was with God, and
> the Word was God. . . . The Word became flesh and made his
> dwelling among us. We have seen his glory, the glory of the One
> and Only, who came from the Father, full of grace and truth.
>
> —John 1:1, 14

> The Son is the radiance of God's glory and the exact representa-
> tion of his being, sustaining all things by his powerful word. After
> he had provided purification for sins, he sat down at the right hand
> of the Majesty in heaven.
>
> —Hebrews 1:3

We could easily add other topics here, such as the virgin birth, the bodily resurrection of Jesus, and other core doctrines, but the point is clear: what we believe matters! If you don't pay close attention to what you believe and what the church you are visiting believes, you can end up in serious trouble.

Many people have joined the Church of Jesus Christ of Latter-Day Saints (whose members are commonly called Mormons) because the group holds high family values. But because they have not taken the time to ask about the group's core beliefs, many new members are unaware that this group believes in many gods, believes humans can evolve into gods, and denies that salvation is based on faith in Jesus alone. Others have joined the Jehovah's Witnesses without knowing that they deny the Trinity and reject other clear teachings in the Bible. Many people join these two groups every year believing that they are Christian churches.

When you are considering a church, be sure to ask about their core beliefs. Many churches can provide a copy of their purpose statement and their statement of faith. In the appendix we have included two statements of faith that have been accepted in Bible-believing Christian churches throughout history. These statements are known as the ecumenical creeds because they are accepted as accurate expressions of biblical faith by Christian churches from a wide variety of backgrounds. We have also included in the appendix a modern statement of faith concerning salvation that you might want to read.

Knowing What Is Core to You

Besides the core beliefs of the Christian faith (those we would never compromise), there are many other beliefs that matter a great deal to Christians but are not essential for salvation. It is helpful to identify the beliefs that are essential in your under-standing of the faith and the beliefs that are important to you but are not core. Anytime the topic of doctrine comes up, there's a risk of someone's being offended, because Christians often dis-agree about which beliefs are core beliefs. Some people have a long list of beliefs they would say are core, while others have a shorter list.

Passionate Christians who are deeply committed to the Bible might disagree on several topics. The point in our discussion is not to declare one perspective right and the other wrong. Our goal is to help you see the importance of knowing where you stand on an issue and where the church stands. The key concern is compatibility.

When a couple comes to our church for premarriage counseling, we use an assessment tool to learn about the couple. This questionnaire, which has over one hundred questions, doesn't measure right and wrong behavior as much as it measures how the couple will get along. For instance, if the woman indicates she wants eleven children and the man indicates he wants one child (or less), trouble might be brewing. If they both want only one child, fine. If they both want a baker's dozen, this is fine also. Knowing where each stands helps the couple avoid big surprises down the road.

In a similar way, knowing what you believe and what a church believes will help you identify points of agreement and disagreement before you say "I do." We have picked a few "big issue" topics as examples of what some Christians might call a core belief and others might not.

The Example of Baptism

Some Christians believe baptism is only for believers and that baptizing infants is wrong. Others have grown up in a church tradition in which infant baptism is a normal part of church life. What happens when a person who has grown up in a church that baptizes only believers moves to a new community and finds a church they really love, only to discover that they baptize infants? Their family fits in at the church, and they feel free to worship God and find joy among God's people there. They believe the Bible is preached, and they like the church. But then they discover that the church baptizes infants.

For many people, this is a core issue. Some people will choose not to be part of a church that baptizes infants, while others value the practice so much that they would not join a church that doesn't believe in it. This can be a hot issue for some people; if it is for you, admit it and be sure to ask the right questions early on in the process.

Other Areas to Consider

Of course, baptism is not the only topic that can create difficulties. Here is a quick look at some other areas worth considering and learning about as you look for a church home.

Some congregations have a specific outlook on *spiritual gifts*. If you come from a background where you expect to see specific manifestations and expressions in a worship service, you would be wise to find out if the church you are visiting has the same outlook. For instance, if you say, "I am looking for a church that openly affirms speaking in tongues," and the church you are visiting does not, you might decide that you need to keep looking.

Another important issue for many people is the *role of women* in the church. Various churches see the role of women in dramatically different ways. Be sure to ask good questions about this topic if you have strong feelings about it.

There are many other issues that can be of concern. What a church believes about *mission work, evangelism, the end times, communion,* and *social action* are just a few examples of areas you might want to look into. Wisdom says you need to identify what beliefs are core or very important to you and take the time to discover what the church believes.

Should I Try to Change My New Church?

Some people will become part of a congregation even after they have identified a key area of disagreement. They may comfort themselves with this thought: "I will assert whatever pressure I can to help this church adopt my way of seeing things." They become part of the church with the goal of changing it to fit their beliefs.

We are not saying that churches should never change. We are also not advocating that people remain silent if the practices or teachings of a church are unbiblical. What we would like to suggest is that joining a church with the intention of changing it might not be the wisest course of action. Becoming part of a congregation when you know you have serious disagreements with their practices and beliefs may not be the best starting point.

If you want to be part of a congregation but walk in the door ready to tell the leaders of First Baptist Church why they should baptize your newborn, you'd better be ready for a fight you have little chance of winning. Coming into a church with this attitude is a recipe for disaster. If your goal, upon joining a church, is to change one of its beliefs, you will probably be in for a short and bumpy ride!

On the other hand, if you begin to connect with a church and see some small differences you can live with, that can be fine. You need to look at any differences you have and ask yourself, "Do I see this as a core belief or as a peripheral issue?" If your disagreement is over a core belief of the faith, it would be best to find another church. If it is over an issue that is not core to your faith, and you feel the church is a good fit, then you are ready to move forward.

Prayer Direction

- Ask God to help you develop a habit of reading the Bible daily so that your beliefs are built on the Bible and tested by the teaching of God's Word.
- Pray for the humility to admit where your beliefs might not be consistent with Scripture and for a willing heart to adjust your beliefs to what the Bible teaches.

For Further Reflection

- What beliefs do you feel are core to your faith?
- What beliefs do you hold dear but feel are not so essential that they would keep you out of a church that sees things differently than you do?

Action You Can Take

Asking the Right Questions

When you visit a church, plan to connect with one of the church leaders (face to face, on the phone, or by e-mail) and ask questions about beliefs that are important to you. Take time to form a list of possible questions. The Beliefs Questionnaire gives you some ideas to get you started. Put a check by questions you feel are important and also add a few of your own in the space provided. If you are in the process of looking for a church as a couple or a family, be sure to have everyone give their input on which questions are important.

BELIEFS QUESTIONNAIRE

☐ What does your church believe about the Bible?

☐ Do you believe Jesus really rose from the dead?

☐ What are your beliefs and practices concerning baptism?

☐ What are your beliefs and practices when it comes to communion (the Lord's Supper/the Eucharist)?

☐ Do you believe in the Trinity?

☐ Do you believe Jesus was God in human flesh?

☐ Do you believe Jesus is God's Son and that salvation comes through faith in him alone?

☐

☐

☐

☐

Understanding the Purpose of the Church

A CHURCH WITHOUT A CLEAR BIBLICAL PURPOSE will wander aimlessly. If you find a church that seems exciting but has no clear purpose, there is a good chance they are vigorously treading water but going nowhere. Activity does not always mean direction or purpose. As you look for a church to call your spiritual home, it is essential to know *why* a particular church exists; what is their *purpose?*

A Purpose-Driven Church

Two thousand years ago Jesus clearly declared his purposes for the church. Since then every truly biblical community of believers has done all they can to fulfill his calling. The purposes Jesus established for us are found in two passages from the Gospel of Matthew. They are often called the Great Commandment (Matt. 22:37–40) and the Great Commission (Matt. 28:19–20). Both come straight from the lips of Jesus:

Jesus replied: "'Love the Lord your God with all your heart and with all your soul and with all your mind.' This is the first and greatest commandment. And the second is like it: 'Love your neighbor as yourself.' All the Law and the Prophets hang on these two commandments."

—Matthew 22:37–40

Therefore go and make disciples of all nations, baptizing them in the name of the Father and of the Son and of the Holy Spirit, and teaching them to obey everything I have commanded you. And surely I am with you always, to the very end of the age.

—Matthew 28:19–20

Although these words were spoken by Jesus two thousand years ago and have been central in the life of the church since the first century, there has been a powerful movement to help congregations organize with clarity around biblical purposes in the last two decades. In his books *The Purpose-Driven Church* and *The Purpose-Driven Life*, Rick Warren tells how Saddleback Church has been organized around the clear biblical purposes laid out in the Great Commandment and the Great Commission and how this vision can impact the lives of those who follow Jesus. He suggests that every church should be built around these biblical purposes, and we agree wholeheartedly.

Five Biblical Purposes

When you read the Great Commandment and the Great Commission and reflect on what they say, you discover that these two passages contain the heartbeat of what the church is supposed to *do* and *be*. Rick Warren and the members of Saddleback Church use five M's to clarify what these passages say about the core purpose of the church:

Magnify: We celebrate God's presence in worship.
Mission: We communicate God's Word through evangelism.
Membership: We incorporate God's family into our fellowship.
Maturity: We educate God's people through discipleship.
Ministry: We demonstrate God's love through service.

These five purposes can be expressed in many different ways. The important thing is to discover whether the church you are connecting with has a clear biblical purpose that includes these essential elements. At the church where we serve and worship, we express God's purpose for the church in this way:

Corinth's Purpose Statement
To *exalt* God through worshiping in Spirit and truth
To *enfold* believers in a loving church family
To *edify* believers through teaching and admonition
To *equip* God's people for ministry
To *evangelize* the unsaved with the Good News of Jesus

A Look at the Purposes

Churches should exist to exalt *God in worship.* When you visit a church, ask yourself if you see a spirit of joy-filled worship. Do the people have a hunger to meet with God and lift him up? Do you feel drawn into the presence of God? Do you sense the Holy Spirit's presence in the worship service? Jesus said, "Yet a time is coming and has now come when the true worshipers will worship the Father in spirit and truth, for they are the kind of worshipers *the Father seeks*" (John 4:23). Jesus wants us to know that the Father is seeking people who will worship him with sincerity and passion. If a church has a commitment to worship, this is a clear sign that they are in tune with the heart of God.

A healthy church will seek to enfold *people into the life of their fellowship.* Open arms and open hearts show that a church values community. The church should be like a body in which all the parts are connected and need each other. In Paul's first letter to the church in the city of Corinth we read, "If one part suffers, every part suffers with it; if one part is honored, every part rejoices with it" (1 Cor. 12:26). We are related, we are connected, and we need to learn how to function as a community of common joy and sorrow. Every part has a unique contribution, and members of the body see their own value but also the importance of the others. The church is like a loving and supportive family. If a church is committed to enfolding people and embracing them in a loving fellowship, this is a strong indicator that their purposes are in line with the Bible.

A church that is in line with God's purposes will seek to edify *the members of the body by helping them grow into full maturity.* The apostle Paul put it in these words: "Then we will no longer be infants, tossed back and forth by the waves, and blown here and there by every wind of teaching and by the cunning and craftiness of men in their deceitful scheming. Instead, speaking the truth in love, we will in all things grow up into him who is the Head, that is, Christ" (Eph. 4:14–15). To express it in simple terms, a church that understands God's purposes will be highly committed to challenging every member to *grow up* in their faith. This kind of purpose-driven church will challenge people to become all God wants them to be. Everyone in the church, from children to adults, should continue to mature in their faith. Look closely at the churches you visit and be sure they have education programs, small groups, and preaching that will create a culture of lifelong spiritual growth.

Another role of the church is to equip *and train all those who attend to grow in their ability to serve God and others.* A church that is on track with biblical purposes will be actively engaged in calling every believer to ministry in the church or the community. This will not be a peripheral issue but a top priority. A church where there is a sense that the pastor alone is responsible for the entire ministry is missing the message of Scripture. God's Word teaches us the role of pastors and teachers, and this role is "to prepare God's people for works of service, so that the body of Christ may be built up" (Eph. 4:12). This is why it is important to find out if a church has a plan for helping members discover, develop, and use their God-given gifts for ministry.

Finally, every church should have a passion for reaching people in their community and the world with the Good News of Jesus through the work of evangelism. After he had risen from the dead, Jesus told his followers, "You will receive power when the Holy Spirit comes on you; and you will be my witnesses in Jerusalem, and in all Judea and Samaria, and to the ends of the earth" (Acts 1:8). The scope of Jesus' mission for his church extends from the closest place (where we live) to the very ends of the earth. As you evaluate the health of a church, look at their heart for the world. Find out whether they are committed to investing time and resources in reaching people with the Good News of salvation that is found in Jesus Christ alone.

If a church has great music, and the people are friendly but they have no clear sense of purpose or direction, be cautious. If a congregation has a beautiful building and the parking lot is full every week, but they don't know why they exist, beware! If a Christian fellowship declares they believe and follow the Bible, but they can't articulate what God has called them to *do* and *be* as a congregation, watch out. A church without purpose might be doing lots of things, but you need to ask, "Are they doing the right things?" As you are looking for a church home, be sure you take the time to discover what a church sees as their primary purpose for existing. Just like a doctor putting a stethoscope to the chest of a patient, the process of learning a church's purpose will help you diagnose its heartbeat.

Prayer Direction

- Thank God for the invitation he has given each of us to worship him. Ask the Holy Spirit to teach you to worship the Father with all your heart.
- Pray for God to show you how you need to be equipped and prepared to serve him and others.

For Further Reflection

- What are some of the signs that might indicate a church is clear about its purpose?
- What are some signs that a church does *not* have a clear purpose and direction?

Action You Can Take

Asking the Right Questions

As you begin to visit churches, plan to connect with one of the church leaders (face to face, on the phone, or by e-mail) and ask some questions about the church's purpose. These questions will help you see whether a church has a clear vision about where they are headed. The Purpose Questionnaire gives you some ideas to get you started.

PURPOSE QUESTIONNAIRE

☐ What do you do as a church to help those who attend grow as worshipers?

☐ How do you help a new member become enfolded in the fellowship and community life of your church?

☐ Do you have a program in place to help a person discover and develop their God-given gifts for ministry?

☐ What do you do to help your church members learn to reach out to others with the love of God and share their faith?

☐

☐

☐

☐

Chapter 4

The Place and Power of Prayer

HOW SERIOUS ARE YOU ABOUT FINDING THE RIGHT CHURCH?
If you are serious about it, you will want to make prayer a
part of the process, every step of the way. Some people pray
regularly. For others, the idea of praying might be a fairly
new concept. If you are looking for a church for the first
time because you have recently begun to wonder about spiritual things, the best first step is prayer. Even if you have
rarely prayed or have never prayed, this is the perfect time to
start. If you are not sure there is a God out there to hear
your prayers, but you want to find out, you might want to
start with a simple prayer something like this:

> *Dear God, I am not sure you are real, but if you are, I want*
> *to know you. I ask also for your help in the process of*
> *finding a church I can love. If your church is really like a*
> *beautiful bride, I want to be part of it. Help me each step of*
> *the way. I pray this in Jesus' name, amen.*

If you are a Christian and prayer is a normal part of your
lifestyle, you will certainly want to begin praying daily for

this process. As you get started, you might want to consider using a prayer like this:

God, I am your child, and I love you. I also know you love me more than I can begin to understand. I ask you to lead and guide me as I look for the right church to call my spiritual home. I am confident there is a local congregation that needs the gifts you have given me, and I need the community and fellowship they will offer. Please help me find the right congregation so I can be an active part of your church. In Jesus' name, amen.

Maybe you have family members who will be greatly affected by the decision you make about which church you will attend. Not only should you invite their input and comments each step of the way, but the process of finding a church could be a great step in helping them see the value and power of prayer. Here is a prayer that could help family members enter into the process:

Dear God, we realize that the process of finding a church for our family is very important. Please help us find a church that will have a place for each of us in the church family. We ask you to lead us to a congregation where people will accept and love us and where we can learn to love them back. Please lead us to a church that will help each one of us grow to love and know you more and help us learn to love each other as well. We pray this in Jesus' name, amen.

God desires to answer our prayers, when they are consistent with his will. Can you imagine how much it will please God to hear you sincerely asking him to lead you to the right church? As you begin praying, know that God wants to answer this prayer even more than you want him to!

This is the confidence we have in approaching God: that if we ask anything according to his will, he hears us. And if we know that he hears us—whatever we ask—we know that we have what we asked of him.

—1 John 5:14–15

Praying Together

If you are searching for a church as a couple or as a family, it is a wonderful time to begin praying together. If you are going to visit a few churches over the course of a couple of months, you might want to commit to pray in the car as you drive to church. Here are some ideas for what you might pray about, whether you are looking for a church on your own, as a couple, or as a family:

- Pray that God will lead you through the process of finding a church home.
- Pray that you (and each person in your family, if you are searching as a family) will be able to worship and praise God as you attend this church. Even if you're not going to end up at this church, the desire of your heart should be to grow as a worshiper.
- Pray for insight concerning the beliefs of the church you are going to visit.
- Remembering that the church is people, pray that you will connect well with the people of this congregation.

After church, again take time to pray:

- Thank God for the experiences you had visiting this congregation.

- Ask God to give you wisdom to know if this might be a church where you could fit in, grow, and serve.

Inviting Others to Pray

In addition to praying on your own or as a family about your search for a church home, it is wise to invite people to pray for you in your journey of finding a church home. There is power in having friends and family members uplift and support you in prayer in this important decision process.

We have an example of the power of prayer support that relates to the book you are holding in your hands. It actually has to do with the chapter you are reading right now. We had been working on this book for over eight months, and things were moving along pretty well. Then, for some reason, we hit a roadblock. The ideas were there, but the words were not flowing onto the page (or more to the point, onto the computer screen). One morning, when we were writing but making slow progress, we sent an e-mail to five friends, asking them to pray for us. We felt we needed some support and knew that this group of people (all of them writers) would pray for us faithfully.

Here is a copy of the e-mail we sent:

We are writing a short note to a few of our friends who know the joys and challenges of writing and hitting deadlines. We are feeling the stress of making a deadline and balancing our writing with the rest of our life responsibilities. We don't hit this point very often, but we are feeling the weight of trying to hit two publishing deadlines that are coming at us pretty quickly.

We would ask for your prayers over the coming month. The church ministry intensifies this time of the year. Along with this, the call to raise three sons who are becoming young men is joyful, but demanding! We are feeling drained and are profoundly aware that we don't have the energy, creativity, or skills to finish these writing projects in our own strength. We are at that wonderful and humbling place where God's strength must come through our weakness or the work won't get done!

Please pray that we will place our trust in him, pour out all the energy and skills he has given us, and that we would finish these writing projects when they are due.

In his amazing grace,
Kevin and Sherry Harney

Since I am mentioning this, I am sure you can guess what happened. At noon that day, about two hours after we had sent this plea for prayer, Sherry and I went out for a lunch date we had planned to talk and pray about our next steps on this book. As we sat and ate lunch at our favorite Chinese restaurant, the wheels just started turning. We spent an hour talking and writing fresh ideas. Stories came to mind that we had not thought about for years! It was as if God launched us into a writing zone.

In the hours of writing that followed, we could feel that God had heard the prayers of our friends. When I got back to my office, I checked my e-mail and had received this note from one of the people we had asked to pray:

Thanks for your email, I will certainly pray daily for you during this time. Please keep me in your prayers also—I'm on deadline for my book THE CASE FOR A CREATOR. I've been making excellent progress in the last week or so, but really need to sustain this for the next 8–12 weeks to finish. I trust you and Sherry and the kids are doing well! God's best to you! Lee

Short, sweet, and what a blessing!

Both Sherry and I are confident that the prayers of Lee and our other friends were a key in our writing process moving forward so well. In the next few hours, we got another e-mail from a prayer partner in Sri Lanka and a call from a friend in California. We found out that three of the five people we had contacted had already been praying for this book. Prayer changes more things than we dream!

Learning the Importance of Prayer Support

Eric and Aimee first visited Corinth Church before either of them was a Christian. They were friendly and were curious about the Christian faith, but they had not made a personal commitment to Jesus Christ. Eric is a college biology teacher, and Aimee is a college math teacher. They are a bright couple that had lots of intellectual questions about the faith.

Over time, through face-to-face discussions and e-mail, many of their questions were answered. Some of their questions were not answered. But along the way—through questions, prayers, attending church, and the gentle work of God's Holy Spirit— Eric and Aimee came to faith in Jesus Christ.

They eventually began to serve in areas of the church that were consistent with their God-given spiritual gifts. They built rich relationships. They grew as worshipers and fell in love with the community of God's people at Corinth Church. Eric and Aimee became part of a small group of couples that we lead in our home on Sunday evenings. Over time, this group of six couples has become good friends. We have studied biblical teachings on marriage and parenting, and our small group of twelve people has become a place of friendship, encouragement, and mutual affirmation.

A few years later Eric and Aimee moved, and their new home was too far from the church for them to keep attending. One of the first things they did when they started the process of looking for a new church was to come to our small group and ask us to pray. We said yes, and we meant it. As of the writing of this book, Eric and Aimee were still coming to our small group and were in the process of looking for a new church home. We were confident that their greatest prayer support is a small group of ten people who don't want to see them go but want God's best for them. We are happy to report that by the time this book was in its final stages, Eric and Aimee had found another church, and they were already loving the new church they had found.

As you move forward in the process of finding a church you can really love, invite others to uphold you in prayer. You will be overjoyed at what a difference it makes. You can also be confident that we have prayed that each person who reads this book will find a church they can love.

Prayer Direction

- Thank God that he hears your prayers and is ready to answer them.
- Pray that you will become courageous in praying with others, especially if this is hard for you.

- Thank God for the people (from your childhood to the present) who have consistently upheld you in prayer.

For Further Reflection

- How have you seen God answer prayers in the past?
- Who is one person you know who lives out a committed prayer life? What can you learn from the example of this person?

Action You Can Take

Using the Bible as Your Prayer Guide

One of the best tools in learning how to pray is to let Scripture guide you. Here are some passages that teach five keys for growing in prayer. These passages will help guide you in the process of finding a church and any time you need God's direction in your life.

1. Ask God to help you.
   Jeremiah 33:3: "*Call to me* and I will answer you and tell you great and unsearchable things you do not know."
   Psalm 32:8: "I will instruct you and teach you in the way you should go; *I will counsel you* and watch over you."

2. Keep in mind the nature of God.
   Matthew 7:7–11: "Ask and it will be given to you; seek and you will find; knock and the door will be opened

to you. *For everyone who asks receives;* he who seeks finds; and to him who knocks, the door will be opened. Which of you, if his son asks for bread, will give him a stone? Or if he asks for a fish, will give him a snake? If you, then, though you are evil, know how to give good gifts to your children, *how much more will your Father in heaven give good gifts to those who ask him!*"

3. Seek God's wisdom and believe that he will lead you.

   James 1:5–8: "If any of you lacks wisdom, *he should ask God,* who gives generously to all without finding fault, and it will be given to him. *But when he asks, he must believe and not doubt,* because he who doubts is like a wave of the sea, blown and tossed by the wind. That man should not think he will receive anything from the Lord; he is a double-minded man, unstable in all he does."

4. Ask in accordance with God's will.

   1 John 5:14–15: "This is the confidence we have in approaching God: *that if we ask anything according to his will, he hears us.* And if we know that he hears us— whatever we ask—we know that we have what we asked of him."

5. Give thanks.

   1 Thessalonians 5:18: "*Give thanks* in all circumstances, *for this is God's will for you* in Christ Jesus."

PART 2

CONNECTING
IN A LOCAL
CONGREGATION

Chapter 5

A Loving Family

OVER THE YEARS, SHERRY and I have traveled to many different parts of the world. From the Netherlands to Mexico, from America to Israel, we have come to a joy-filled realization: we have family everywhere! It is astounding how quickly we connect with people who have no blood relationship to us. We have been invited into the homes of Christians in Switzerland and France and have felt right at home because we are family to each other. Our basement has been converted into a guest apartment because we have spiritual family all over the world, and they know our home is open to them when they are in town. We have been overjoyed again and again with the realization that our family ties go much deeper than blood. We are part of God's family.

A Forever Family

When we become part of a church, we enter a family relationship that will impact not only this life but eternity.

Through Jesus Christ, we are adopted into his forever family. The Bible is filled with examples of God's understanding of the church as a spiritual family. The passages below give a biblical perspective on God's plan to form a family of faith.

> Yet to all who received him, to those who believed in his name, he gave the right to become children of God—children born not of natural descent, nor of human decision or a husband's will, but born of God.
>
> —John 1:12–13

> He [Jesus] replied to him, "Who is my mother, and who are my brothers?" Pointing to his disciples, he said, "Here are my mother and my brothers. For whoever does the will of my Father in heaven is my brother and sister and mother."
>
> —Matthew 12:48–50

> Let us not become weary in doing good, for at the proper time we will reap a harvest if we do not give up. Therefore, as we have opportunity, let us do good to all people, especially to those who belong to the family of believers.
>
> —Galatians 6:9–10

God longs to forge his people into a loving and healthy family unit. This family includes people of every nation, every social group, and every walk of life. When we are born into our earthly family, we don't get to choose our parents or siblings. It is the same when we enter the family of God. We inherit a family, and God's plan is to form our lives and character through relationship with our spiritual family members.

The Joy of Having Two Families

I was born into a wonderful family with a dad and mom, three sisters, and one brother. I love each one of them and celebrate every opportunity I have to spend time with them. I share a closeness with them because we have a common history, a common story, a common love. Sherry's family includes her dad and mom, a brother, and a sister. It is a joy to gather with her family on holidays and special occasions because of the warmth we experience when we are with them. Both Sherry and I are thankful to God for our families.

Yet God has given us a bonus in this life. He has given us another family. As followers of Christ and members of the church, we have been adopted into God's spiritual family.

We all have a birth family, but when we come to faith in Christ, we become part of another family, a spiritual family that will last forever. When we join this family, we inherit countless brothers and sisters, parents, and even spiritual children. The apostle Paul puts it this way:

> Long ago, even before he made the world, God loved us and chose us in Christ to be holy and without fault in his eyes. His unchanging plan has always been to adopt us into his own family by bringing us to himself through Jesus Christ. And this gave him great pleasure.
>
> —Ephesians 1:4–5 NLT

Our new spiritual family offers tremendous benefits as well as many challenges. As God's family, the church should be a place of harmony and encouragement. But just like in our birth families, there can be conflicts and times of tension. When we aren't careful, our relationships can become strained and tense. Just because we are part of God's spiritual family doesn't mean we are guaranteed relational bliss. We must work at building strong and life-giving relationships. In our earthly family and in our spiritual family, we quickly discover that we must either build good relationships or settle for less. God's desire is for us to invest in building healthy relationships in our birth family and in our church family. Both matter to him!

In the church we meet our new family, the family of God. The church provides fathers, mothers, sons, daughters, brothers, and sisters who will encourage, love, and even challenge us. Both Sherry and I have many stories to tell about people who have loved us and have become family through our relationship with them in the church. Through our history in the church, we have learned why God has provided the gift of a spiritual family.

A Family in Times of Joy

One beautiful picture of spiritual family love is a couple in our congregation. Dan and Lori have helped in the youth ministry of our church over the past twenty years. They have been friends, teachers, and even spiritual parents to many of our teens. This couple has spent countless hours listening to young people as they process life's pains and joys. They have been on mission trips and adventure trips all over the country. They have been family to the students in our church, and the students have been family to them. I have seen God's love and joy in many ways as this couple has discovered they are not part of some organization that meets once or twice a week; they are part of the church, God's family!

Another picture of spiritual family love is a woman that everyone in our church calls Grandma Lois. She makes a point of trying to meet and greet every new visitor who comes to the church. Grandma Lois is a hugger; she warmly embraces visitors (if they are willing) and hundreds of children, teens, and adults *every week*. Even when someone has been coming to our church for just a few weeks, they receive a welcome just like any other church family member. Grandma Lois gives joy through her hugs and words of affirmation, but she also receives many blessings along the way.

Anyone who decides to be part of a healthy church will discover great joy. In the family of faith, we can laugh, play, and celebrate life together. Knowing that your family members are ready to rejoice with you in times of victory and comfort you in times of sorrow brings a sense of security and hope!

A Family in Times of Sorrow and Need

When Kevin and I were first married and when we had our first son, we were living in California. Because neither of our families lived very close to us, our church family became a huge source of connectedness and care. People in the congregation of New Hope Church loved us and adopted us as family. One couple in particular, Walt and Patty, adopted Kevin and me and our son, Zach. Their daughter, Michelle, was Zach's first babysitter. On birthdays and holidays, Walt, Patty, and Michelle were always there. To this day, sixteen years later, Walt and Patty still send cards and gifts to all three of our boys, and when we are anywhere near their town in California, we always stop in to see them. When we moved to Michigan, it was just as hard to say goodbye to them as it was to blood relatives.

The summer after we moved to Michigan, Walt and Patty came to visit. While they were with us, Michelle was in a car accident. She was hit by a man who had been drinking. Michelle never recovered from the accident. Walt and Patty flew home that night, and we were on a plane forty-eight hours later to be with them. Kevin would do the funeral. We cried with them. We prayed with them. We sat with them in the car leading the funeral procession. We shared stories about this terrific young Christian girl and how painful it was to say goodbye. Through our tears, we discovered that the family of God is a community of strength and comfort, even in life's greatest tragedies.

God does not want us to walk through this life alone. He has provided a haven, a safe harbor for the storms of life. It is called the church, the family of God. When you connect in the life of a congregation, you will be the recipient of care and comfort on many occasions. You will also be able to share love with others and care for those who are suffering and going through times of loss and sorrow. This is part of what it means to be a part of God's family.

> Praise be to the God and Father of our Lord Jesus Christ, the Father of compassion and the God of all comfort, who comforts us in all our troubles, so that we can comfort those in any trouble with the comfort we ourselves have received from God.
>
> —2 Corinthians 1:3–4

Identifying Signs of Healthy Family Life

As you search for a church that functions like a healthy family, there are a number of things to look for. First, take note of how people get along. Do they seem to enjoy being with each other? Is there a buzz and joy in the air? Are people talking, laughing, and smiling? Think about a holiday family gathering and how you feel when you walk in the door. Excitement fills the house and you can feel the love! A church that is functioning as a healthy family will have this kind of feeling.

Families should have an open-arms policy; when you are family, you are welcome. Take note of how people greet you at the church you are visiting. First impressions say a great deal. As you visit the church additional times, notice if people say hello to you. Do they go out of their way to make you feel at home? Do you get the immediate sense that people are glad you are there?

When a family is functioning right, the members like to be together. In the church family this includes regular worship but should also include more than the hour-long Sunday meeting. Discover if the church provides opportunities to gather for fun and relationship-building experiences. Do they have small groups in which you can experience the church family in a more intimate setting? Does the church make efforts to connect people to each other?

As you look for a church, be sure to identify signs of vital family life. If you find a church that functions as a healthy spiritual family, you will feel it! You will find yourself drawn to these people because all of us desire a place where we know we are loved and where we belong.

Prayer Direction

- Take time to pray for people you know who are going through a painful time. Pray for God's comfort to come to them. Also, pray for the ability to see how you can help extend God's care to them in the coming days.
- If you are facing some kind of tension in a relationship with a family member (in either your birth family or your spiritual family), pray for reconciliation. Pray for a humble heart that is ready to confess any wrong you have done and for the ability to forgive those who have wronged you.

For Further Reflection

- What is one time a person or a group of people from God's family came alongside you when you were hurting, and how did their presence and care help you?
- Once you find a church you love and connect in the life of this church, how might you extend care and support to people who are going through a time of sorrow and loss?
- What are some signs you can look for to see if a church is functioning as a healthy family?

Action You Can Take

A Word of Thanks

Identify a person in your birth family who has been a source of strength and encouragement in your life and find a way to communicate your appreciation to them. You might want to write a note, make a phone call, get them a small gift, or take them to lunch. Whatever you do, be sure to let them know how much they mean to you. If you have been part of a church in the past, consider doing the same thing with one of the members of your spiritual family.

Understanding the Family (Matters of Style)

Sometimes you just see it coming! A couple meets and "falls madly in love." They are sure they're the perfect fit, so they rush toward marriage. They are hopelessly optimistic and are positive their relationship will endure, no matter what everyone else says!

Everyone who knows this couple sees what they cannot. Because they are so different, so dramatically incompatible, all their friends and family members start giving them warnings from the first day: Slow down! Take your time! Get to know each other. Have a few counseling sessions. Meet with a pastor and talk about this decision before you rush forward.

After the wedding, things get tough. The incompatibility issues rise to the surface, and conflict follows. Sometimes this conflict is subtle, under the surface. At other times it explodes, and everyone can see the signs of trouble. Either way, tension mounts and things start to come apart. Sometimes it takes years. Sometimes it takes only weeks or months. In severe cases, the first eruption of this sleeping volcano occurs during the honeymoon.

This is not to say that people who are very different can't have wonderful and fulfilling marriages. However, when a couple rushes into a marriage relationship believing that their emotional passion will be enough to make things work over the long haul, they are often headed for trouble. When a couple presses forward in their relationship without reflecting deeply on their differences and their compatibility, they could be facing some tough days ahead. If a couple believes that ignoring dramatic personality differences will make the differences go away, they have some huge life lessons to learn.

In a similar way, people can find themselves in a bad church situation if they do not address how their preferred style of worship and the church's style of worship fit together (or don't fit). This chapter is not meant to encourage narcissism. Rather, it is a call for an honest acknowledgment that style matters. You can find a church that has rock-solid, biblical beliefs, but it still might not be the right church for you because your style and the style of the church are so different. Some people visit a church and decide they like it but fail to look closely at how the style of the church meshes with their personal style. When they begin to realize that they stick out at this church, they must then decide if they are going to adjust their personal style, continue feeling like a misfit, or move on to a new church. This chapter, and the one that follows, will help you think through the issue of worship style on a number of levels. We will continue to remind you that the primary goal isn't to find a church that matches you perfectly; no such church exists. The goal is to find a church where you are free to worship, grow, and serve without running into constant feelings that you don't fit in.

The Other Side of the Coin

Couples who enter a marriage relationship with their eyes wide open tend to do much better over the long haul. They identify similarities and build on them, which builds strength into the marriage. Newlyweds who clearly see their differences and discover ways to live with them have a much better chance of having a healthy, joy-filled, and life-giving marriage.

Over the years, we have watched many couples enter a dating relationship and move toward marriage with a clear sense that they have a great deal in common and that they are committed to work at building a strong marriage. In a world where so many who say "I do" end up in divorce court, couples that start with a higher level of compatibility have a better chance of weathering the relational storms they will undoubtedly face. This doesn't mean that high levels of compatibility are a guarantee that the marriage will last, but it certainly increases the odds.

We have seen this pattern in the church. Those who come in with their eyes open, having made the effort to find a church that has a high level of compatibility in beliefs and style, tend to connect on a deeper level. They tend to stay longer. These people can often say with enthusiasm, "I have found a church I really love!"

Take Your Time

There is not a 100 percent parallel between the dynamics of a marriage relationship and what happens when someone joins a church family, but there are many similarities. Rushing into joining a church and rushing into a marriage relationship can have similar consequences. But in both cases, taking your time, building a relationship, and evaluating similarities and differences can help the process go much more smoothly.

Over the years, we have watched people join the church, connect with other followers of Jesus, build rich relationships, and find a rich sense of community. These people quickly develop a sense of belonging and joy over being part of the church. They learn what it means to be part of a church not only in terms of attending but also serving, worshiping, and reaching out to those who don't yet know the amazing love of God.

We have also seen people who come to the church and jump in with both feet without reflecting deeply on their personal style and the style of the church. They don't take the time to ask the tough compatibility questions. Some of these people rush into joining the church and even volunteer to serve in a ministry. Then in a short time they disappear. When someone from the church contacts them and asks why they are no longer attending, it is almost never a matter of beliefs or doctrine. It is rarely a matter of not feeling accepted or welcomed, because they do! In ten years of ministry at our church, not one person has reported that they left because they felt they weren't needed or because they couldn't find a place to serve. The vast majority of the time the reason given is a matter of style! This is why we have chosen to focus on this issue so intensely.

Why do some people connect in a church and fall in love with it, while others end up leaving in a short time? The primary reason is that some people are very thoughtful and prayerful about the church-search process and ask good questions about the church's beliefs and style. Others feel an initial attraction, join the church, and then discover differences they just can't seem to reconcile. In time they move on to a new church, often with the same results.

We have learned to encourage people to take at least a month or two to make any firm decision about joining a specific congregation. As a matter of practice, if someone visits our church for the first or second time and tells one of the pastors that they are planning to join, we encourage them to take their time. We see the need for people to do their homework and think deeply about this decision, even when it comes to our own church.

Not Better, Not Worse . . . Just Different

This isn't about being consumers; it is simply about finding the church that is the best fit for us. Not all churches are the same. Some have a highly traditional style of worship with strict adherence to the liturgy, while others have a very informal and freeflowing worship style. Some churches use keyboards, electric guitars, and drums to lead worship singing, and others prefer an organ leading hymns. Some congregations encourage a broad spectrum of expressions during the worship service such as raising hands, shouts of joy, and even dancing, while others lean toward more subdued expressions (if any expression at all). And other churches seek to blend various worship styles and extend a hand of welcome to people from many different backgrounds.

Maybe You Should Visit a Few Other Churches

When a person or family visits the church where we serve, our church members are careful not to work too hard at getting them to join the church or even to commit to staying. Our first concern is not that they become part of Corinth Church; we want them to discover if our church is where God wants them to be. The last thing we want is for them to come to our church if it is not the right church for them.

Some people reading these words will protest and say, "Wait a minute, can't anyone attend and fit into any church?" The answer is, Yes! And the answer is, No! We would say that any Christian can gather with any other group of believers and have a great sense of fellowship and a meaningful worship experience. At the same time, if his or her personal style is dramatically different than the style of the church, over time this can create tensions. We will look at this in greater detail in the next chapter.

Here is an example that might surprise you. When a family visits Corinth Church and I get a chance to meet them, I will often ask questions like, "How did you end up visiting Corinth Church?" Most often the answer is that they were invited by someone who already attends the church. I will also ask, "What do you think of the church so far?" They will usually talk about the warmth of the people and their impressions of our worship services or our education ministry. In most cases, their comments are positive.

Yet there are times when someone will say, "I enjoyed the service, but it felt too informal to me." I will ask them what they mean, specifically. They might say something like, "Well, in the church I came from, we said the Lord's Prayer on a weekly basis and had the reading of the Law. I noticed you missed those things." They might then follow up with, "In my old church, we didn't have guitars and drums." At this point in the conversation I might ask them how important these practices are to them. How much do they value these expressions? Are these aspects of a worship service essential for them to truly enjoy worship?

If they say these practices are deeply important to them, I will usually tell them about a couple of churches in our community that are solidly biblical but much more traditional. There are two congregations in close driving distance to our church that I often refer people to if they are looking for a more traditional worship experience. One of these is in the same denomination as the church I serve; the other is not. But both are biblical churches that have a much more traditional style of worship, music, and dress.

When I tell people they might want to visit a few other churches in our community, I almost always get the same look of puzzlement and shock. My observation is that people have an innate sense that every pastor wants to do anything it takes to get new people to stay at their church. If this is the case, the pastors at our church certainly break the mold. We want people to be in the right church. If that is Corinth, great! If it is another Bible-believing fellowship of Christians, that's great too.

Once people get over the shock of being told they might want to visit other churches, I sometimes jokingly say, "I don't get bonuses or commissions on new members. My goal isn't to convince you to come to this church." I always follow up by assuring them that my prayer is that they find the right church, a church they can really love. Once people understand that our concern is for their spiritual growth and health, it begins to make sense to them. Many of the visitors I have had this conversation with end up staying at Corinth or coming back after a number of weeks attending elsewhere. If they do come back, they do so knowing that we are committed to our style of worship and that they need to be ready to live without some of the stylistic expressions they have loved in the past.

Being Honest about Differences

One of our seminary professors, C. Peter Wagner, once asked a group of students, "When is the best time to have an unhappy church member move on from your church?" We offered a few ideas, but then he gave us his answer: "Before they join!" This might seem harsh and unwelcoming, but we all understood the spirit with which he spoke. Peter was always sensitive and caring. He taught with excitement, and it was impossible to miss the fact that he wanted all of us to become leaders in churches that gave a great deal of attention to keeping the church doors wide open for everyone.

The point Peter was making had to do with style. He knew that if someone was going to become part of a local church, they needed to be part of the right church. He knew that not every congregation will fit every person. But God in his wisdom has given us Bible-believing churches that express the same faith in different ways. We need to celebrate these various stylistic expressions and embrace them. We also need to be honest about our differences and help people find the right church for them.

Our worship style at Corinth Church is fairly contemporary and informal. If someone is looking for a worship service where the pastors wear flowing robes, enter in procession, or pray in King James English, our church will not hit the spot for them. If they are looking for a service where the organ will blow their hair back and the hymns are sung on a weekly basis, they will be disap-

pointed. If they are expecting a formal order of worship that doesn't change from week to week, they will be frustrated. Our pastors wear suits on occasion, but we often dress casually. Our church is becoming less formal and less traditional as the years pass. This is not right or wrong; it is simply where we are in terms of worship style.

At Corinth, we require prospective members to take a four-hour class before joining the church. In this class, we are unapologetic about our church's practices, including matters of style. We want people to know that if style is a big issue to them, if it will keep them from feeling free to worship, if it will be a point of irritation and contention, they ought to consider looking at other churches. We take the style issue that seriously!

"Church Shopping"

In recent years, many people have begun to use the term "church shopping" to refer to the process of finding a church home. This term can be harmless when used to refer to the process of trying to find the right church where they can grow, worship, experience community, and serve. But the term is troublesome when it reflects the consumeristic attitude of trying to find a church that will meet their every need and make them happy! If we go out looking for a church with the idea that we want to find a place that will always give us everything we need, we will find ourselves on an endless "shopping" trip.

People who see the church as a vendor of spiritual goods that exists to meet their every spiritual whim and fancy are going to be disappointed. There are no perfect churches because the church is made up of people, and there are no perfect people. But if shopping, or looking, for a church home is about finding a place that teaches God's Word with integrity and that helps us worship and grow in a way that fits who we are, this can be a joyful and healthy process, no matter what term we use to describe it.

When looking for a church you can really love, it is important to ask some basic questions about worship style. These questions can be asked in advance through a simple phone call or a quick e-mail and can be easily answered by a church attendee. Many of your style-related questions can be also answered through personal observation by making one visit to a church.

We need to be clear about priorities. Style should *not* be the primary issue when seeking to find a church we can love. If you look at style but miss the substance (the beliefs, doctrines, and practices of the church), you might find yourself in a church with a style that feels right but with beliefs that are not biblical! This would be a horrible mistake. But on the other hand, if you look only at the substance of a church's beliefs and fail to take into account the worship style of the church, you might soon discover that while you affirm the beliefs of the church you are attending, you will feel like a fish out of water every time you go to worship. Stylistic differences can matter more than we think.

Prayer Direction

- Pray for the insight to identify some of the characteristics God has placed in you and how they will fit with various kinds of churches.
- Praise God for inviting diverse styles and expressions into his church, and pray for God's blessing on all of his congregations, all over the world, no matter what their style of worship.

For Further Reflection

- Are you drawn toward a formal or informal style of worship service?
- What style of music helps you sing with the greatest level of focus on God, and why does this musical style help connect you to God?

Action You Can Take

Asking the Right Questions

As you begin to visit churches, plan to connect with one of the church leaders (face to face, on the phone, or by e-mail) and ask some questions about their worship style. The Worship Style Questionnaire on the next two pages might help you think of style issues that are important to you.

WORSHIP STYLE QUESTIONNAIRE

☐ How would you describe your worship service? Is it formal or informal? (You might even ask if they have a printed order of worship. If they do, you can ask if they would mail you the orders from the past two weeks.)

☐ Are there certain elements that appear in the worship service every week (such as the Lord's Prayer, the Apostle's Creed, or the reading of the Law)?

☐ What kind of songs do you sing in your services?

☐ What kind of instruments are used in your services?

☐ To blend in at your church, what would a man wear and what would a woman wear?

☐

☐

☐

☐

Here are some optional questions that might be a little more challenging:

☐ If I shouted "Amen!" during the sermon because I really agreed with something, would people stare at me?

☐ If I raised my hands during worship, would I stand out in the crowd?

☐ If I came to your church six weeks in a row, would I be able to memorize your order of worship or would you still have some surprises for me?

☐ My kids live in jeans and T-shirts; would they feel at home at your church?

☐

☐

☐

☐

One Family,
Many Tastes

IN CHAPTER 6, we looked at how much style matters when it comes to finding a church family. In this chapter, we will look at four specific elements of style that seem to impact a person's ability to connect in a particular church. Again, we want to emphasize that personal tastes are not the primary concern when it comes to worship. God is on the throne, and he is the center of worship. God deserves our praise and adoration. Issues of style are important mainly because if we are constantly distracted and unable to worship, this dishonors God. We need to find a church where we are released to lift up heartfelt, Spirit-filled worship to God.

In the coming pages we will look at the following aspects of style:

- The general style of a worship service
- The style of music used in worship
- Outward expressions (dancing, shouting, etc.) of worship
- The clothing style (formal or informal) of the church members

We are aware that some who read this chapter will argue that none of these things should matter. They will insist that a mature Christian can worship in any church, no matter what the style. We would be quick to agree!

We have worshiped with brothers and sisters who express their praise in styles different than what is normal for us. We have gathered with followers of Christ in various parts of the United States and the world and have attended services in different languages and with radically different styles. In these gatherings, we have been freed to glorify and exalt God. But we would also have to say that certain styles of worship usher us into God's presence more naturally. When choosing a church, it is important to realize that some styles of worship may distract you and hinder you in your worship, while other styles will lead you naturally into God's presence. This will make more sense as you read the examples in this chapter.

The Style of a Worship Service

One style issue to consider is the formality of a worship service. Some congregations have a more formal worship style. The service has a clearly established order, and you always know what is coming next. Worshipers who prefer a formal worship style often find peace and comfort in knowing that the order won't change much from week to week. Many people have a real love for a familiar and consistent order to the worship service. It helps them draw near to God.

Other congregations have a more free-flowing order of worship. The service might change each week, so many churches do not use a printed order of the service. In some churches, the worship leaders are not entirely sure when they will be going in the service because they feel called to wait and see how the Holy Spirit leads them. Some people find this kind of service exciting and invigorating and that it does a great deal to facilitate worship for them. The free-flowing movement and spontaneity lead them into God's presence.

For every person who loves structure and predictability in a worship service, there is another person who finds this kind of routine stagnant and boring. After a few weeks or months of a familiar format, they find themselves distracted and struggling to worship. The familiar format that helps one person worship is a stumbling block for another.

Neither extreme in formality is more "spiritual." Neither is right or wrong. Being formal or informal is not a sign of spiritual maturity; the services are simply different. The key is to identify which style most naturally ushers you into the presence of God and brings you to a place of adoration.

Countless congregations are somewhere in between these two extremes of worship style. Most churches use a mixture of informal and formal elements. Even a church that does not have a printed order of the service can have a fairly familiar feel and consistency to the flow of worship.

The church we serve and attend leans toward the more informal end of the worship style continuum, but we are certainly more formal than many churches. This hit home for us around Christmas the year after we had planted a new congregation. After two years of praying, planning, and developing a core group, Corinth Church launched a new ministry about fifteen minutes away from our church. This new congregation, Wayfarer Community Church, began with about fifty people and had grown to around a hundred in less than a year.

We were able to attend the first Christmas service at Wayfarer. Although Corinth Church is more informal than many congregations, Wayfarer is more relaxed in their style. This is not unusual for new church starts. Near the end of the service, the pastor looked at the congregation and said, "Does anyone have anything to share with the rest of us?" He invited people to communicate prayer needs, words of praise to God, affirmations of blessing for others in the church, or whatever was on their hearts. For the next ten minutes, about eight or nine people responded to this invitation. It seemed natural and fit their worship context.

This works well at Wayfarer. It might not work as well at another church. It is critical that we don't label these different approaches as good or bad. If the Bible is taught and the believers are growing and reaching out to others with God's love, both formal and informal church services can be deeply meaningful and accomplish God's purpose in our lives.

Musical Style

No specific style of music is more spiritual or better than any other, no matter how loudly some might disagree or protest. Some people are certain there will be a huge pipe organ in heaven, and others are sure that the heavenly singing will be led by electric guitars. Some live with a personal assurance that God loves classical music, and others just know that his passion is gospel music. Some people are stirred to worship when they hear a great hymn of the church played by a piano, flute, and violin trio, or on a pipe organ.

Others find themselves launched into the presence of God by an electric guitar, bass, and drums being played as loudly as possible.

Who is right? What kind of music does God enjoy most? Shouldn't Christians be just fine with any kind of music if it has words that honor God? This is a debate that will continue until we go to heaven and find out that God has much broader musical tastes than we have ever dreamed! In the book of Psalms, we hear this invitation:

> Praise him with the sounding of the trumpet,
>   praise him with the harp and lyre,
> praise him with tambourine and dancing,
>   praise him with the strings and flute,
> praise him with the clash of cymbals,
>   praise him with resounding cymbals.
> Let everything that has breath praise the LORD.
> Praise the LORD.
>
> —Psalm 150:3–6

As we read this psalm, and other passages like it, we get the distinct impression that God loves all kinds of music!

In this world, we will have to live with the reality that most of us don't have the breadth of musical taste and appreciation that God does. Even though God can enjoy worship lifted up by sincere hearts in many styles, we might not be as eclectic. For most of us, musical style does matter. This does not mean we can't enter into worship if the music is not to our liking, but a steady diet of worship music that we find abrasive does not help to foster a spirit of praise.

Many people tend to gravitate toward a church where the music connects for them and facilitates worship. If someone becomes a follower of Christ, and they have always loved classical music, it is unlikely they will join a church that has music led by hard-core rock musicians. By the same token, to those who grew up on rock music and love that kind of instrumentation, the classical sound might not connect for them. This isn't to say that people can't, and don't, cross over in their musical styles when it comes to worship, but most people will look for a church that has a musical style they enjoy. As you are looking for a church you can really love, the issue of musical style is a legitimate consideration. It should not be the first consideration, or even the main issue, but it is important to think about.

What do you do if you have various musical tastes in your family? This might mean looking for a church that offers musical breadth. Many churches that are biblical in their teaching and vibrant in their worship offer a varied or blended musical style. Other churches have multiple services offering the same sermon with different musical styles. There are even emerging churches that have worship complexes with multiple gathering places where diverse musical styles are offered but everyone views the same sermon through video. As a family, it will be helpful to take into account what kind of music helps each member of the family go deeper as a worshiper.

One final note we must all keep in mind. Worship is not first and foremost about our stylistic preferences; it is about giving God glory and praise. It is about coming into his presence and exalting and worshiping him. So if the musical style of the worship service facilitates passionate worship, it is an important concern. At the same time, if the musical style makes it almost impossible for you to focus on God and give him praise, this is a concern as well.

Expressiveness in Worship

Another area in which sincere followers of Jesus have dramatic differences in worship style is the way they express themselves. Many Bible-believing and passionate worshipers are quiet and reserved in their expressions, while many others are outward and demonstrative in their worship expression. For some Christians, dancing, jumping, and shouting are natural responses in a worship service. For others, these expressions could be a real distraction. The Bible invites and allows many kinds of expressiveness in worship. Here are some examples:

- Singing (Eph. 5:19)
- Dancing (Ex. 15:20 and 2 Sam. 6:14–15)
- Lifting of hands (Ps. 63:4 and 1 Tim. 2:8)
- Kneeling (Ps. 95:6)
- Lying prostrate (flat on our faces or flat on our backs) (2 Chron. 20:18)
- Shouting for joy (Ps. 33:3)

The question here is not whether God calls us to be active in our worship. It is clear that this can and should be a normal part of our worship. But it is fair to ask yourself if you are freed to worship by the level of expressiveness of those around you or if you feel distracted and hindered in your worship.

When Kevin and I were first married, we would sometimes attend a church in California that was open to many expressions of worship. Some people were kneeling in the aisles, others were standing with hands lifted, and others were sitting and joining in the songs that were being lifted in praise. It just so happened that we were seated just one row in front of a woman who felt very free to express herself through praying out loud through the whole service. Her prayers were loud enough for people to hear many rows away, but to those directly in front of her, it sounded like she was shouting. For me, this freedom of expression became a distraction.

This did not mean we never worshiped in this congregation again; it just meant we were careful to find a seat away from those who were highly verbal. For both of us, this level of expressiveness on the part of someone else actually kept us from worshiping. The key is to realize that different Christians express themselves in dramatically different ways. It is not a matter of one way being right and another way being wrong; they are just different. A great example of differences in expression is found in Second Chronicles. The people of Israel were under attack by a far superior military force, and they were fearful! They knew there was no way they could win a battle against this enemy. So they cried out to God in prayer. They asked for him to intervene on their behalf—and that is exactly what God did! God promised the people he would be with them and they would not be defeated. This is what God said to the people:

> You will not have to fight this battle. Take up your positions; stand firm and see the deliverance the LORD will give you, O Judah and Jerusalem. Do not be afraid; do not be discouraged. Go out to face them tomorrow, and the LORD will be with you.
>
> —2 Chronicles 20:17

How do you respond to hope-filled, joyful news from God? You worship the one who has promised to deliver you from your enemy. But how do you worship? What is the appropriate posture or expression? Just look at how the people responded in worship:

> Jehoshaphat bowed with his face to the ground, and all the people of Judah and Jerusalem fell down in worship before the LORD. Then some Levites from the Kohathites and Korahites stood up and praised the LORD, the God of Israel, with very loud voice.
>
> —2 Chronicles 20:18–19

Wait a minute. What is going on here?

All the people have heard the same good news. They all follow the same God. But some of them bowed down in humble reverence while others jumped to their feet and started shouting praises to God. There were two dramatically different responses to God's promise of deliverance.

Who was right, the humble bowers or the enthusiastic shouters? The answer is simple. Both groups were right! There is not a right and wrong way to worship. As long as we are seeking to honor God and are sensitive to those around us, we are free to express ourselves in the many and various ways the Bible encourages.

At the same time, we need to admit that each of us has a certain temperament and wiring that make different levels of expressiveness either helpful or distracting. The expressions are not right or wrong, but the way we express ourselves in worship will have an impact on which church we choose.

Some people would have a difficult time worshiping in a church where no one lifts their hands or shows much outward expression. They would want to lift their hands, stand up, and shout "Amen!" Yet in some church settings, such expressions would seem out of place. It might even become a distraction to other worshipers because they are not used to this level of expression in a worship service. A person who feels natural dancing, jumping, and shouting during a worship service might want to think twice before joining a church where these expressions are foreign. Although the church where we serve is open to outward expressions during worship, we had the limits of this openness tested some years ago when a new couple joined. I'll let Kevin tell the story.

Free to Do Anything in Worship?

Some years ago we had a couple join our church. The wife came from a church background that was more physically and verbally expressive than our church. Soon after they began attending, she began to realize that she felt confined in her expressions, and some of the worshipers around her were feeling a little distracted by her freedom. She is a wonderful Christian woman, so we had a great conversation about the situation and put everything on the table.

I remember saying to her, "In some churches, people feel free to dance down the aisles during the singing time." She said, with great enthusiasm, "I would love to do that!" I then asked a simple question: "What do you think people at this church would be doing if you were dancing down the aisles?" She responded with great insight, "Many of them would be staring at me!" I agreed and then asked, "If their eyes and minds are on you, who is the focal point of worship?" She said, "I guess it would be me and not God."

This conversation happened some years ago, but it is still fresh in my mind. This dear woman and I agreed that there are churches in our area where dancing in the aisles would *not* be a distraction.

This practice is normal in some churches and is seen as a natural part of worship. In these churches, dancing in the aisles is a perfectly appropriate expression. We also agreed that God wants to be the center of worship. So when she is at Corinth, she is sensitive to the other worshipers and does not express herself in ways that would be distracting.

As we processed this practical and sensitive issue of expressiveness in gathered worship settings, I remembered a couple of quotes my dad was fond of reciting as I was growing up. They are both about the way that living in community with others curtails our personal freedom. He attributed both quotes to Oliver Wendell Holmes Jr., the U.S. Supreme Court justice. The first is, "Our freedom of speech ends when someone yells 'fire' in a crowded theater." The other quote that always stuck with me was, "Our freedom to extend our arm ends where the nose of the person standing next to us begins." In short, our freedoms, in every area of life, are limited when we are with other people; this includes worship.

As you look for a church you can really love, you need to be sensitive to how you express yourself in worship and take this into account. This doesn't mean you can't adjust and adapt to a new church home, but it does mean you need to be aware that how you worship and how others worship has an impact on worshipers around you.

Clothing Styles

As we worked on this chapter, Sherry and I discussed whether we even wanted to include this section on clothing styles. It seems like such a small thing. Should it really matter? We are always happy to report to people that there is no dress code at our church. "Come dressed in what feels right for you." But as we talked about it, Sherry reminded me about an experience I had when I visited a church some years ago. This story might put things into context.

Every year I have a few Sundays when I have no responsibilities at my church and I am not out of town. On these days, I like to visit other churches in the greater Grand Rapids area. There are a lot of strong, Bible-teaching congregations in the area, and I like to drop in so I can worship with God's people, and so I can remember what it feels like to come into a new church as a visitor.

My personal clothing preference, when I can have my way, is sweat pants or jeans and a T-shirt. When I'm not compelled to dress up, I prefer casual attire. So when I visit other churches, I tend to wear my jeans. I do this for two reasons. First, I feel most comfortable in casual clothes. Second, I am curious how I will be received at a church if I come dressed down. Will I be warmly accepted or snubbed?

One Sunday, I decided to visit a local church that I had looked forward to attending. Dressed in my casual attire of jeans and a T-shirt, I approached the front door, ready to meet the woman greeting people entering the church. I smiled and greeted her. She glared at me sourly, looked me up and down from head to toe, and then extended an insincere greeting. She never smiled and never extended a hand for shaking.

As I walked past her, I thought to myself, "I just got snubbed!" It felt bad. But then I thought, maybe she is like this with everyone. Maybe she is one of those people who don't smile much and aren't naturally warm. I wondered if possibly she had been placed in the wrong ministry and did not know how to greet people. So I walked into the entry area and turned around to watch her greet a few other people.

The next few people that came through the door were greeted with smiles, warm welcomes, and handshakes. It was like she was a different person. I also noticed that all those who came in were adhering to a fairly common dress code. The women wore dresses that were semiformal. The men wore suits or nice slacks and dress shirts. No one else was in jeans and a T-shirt. I had been snubbed! The good news was that when I got inside the worship center, two other people were quite friendly and treated me with kindness and dignity.

Some churches operate with an unwritten dress code. When you walk in, you can figure it out in about two seconds. All churches should accept anyone, no matter how they dress, and most churches do, but there is still a sense of what is normative. If a person wants to wear sandals, shorts, and a T-shirt to church, and they choose a congregation where everyone else is dressed very formally, they just need to be ready to stick out.

A church Sherry and I attended in California had a flexible and casual feeling when it came to clothing. The preaching pastor always wore Hawaiian shirts (and never a tie). He would wear casual slacks and sometimes even wore sandals. As you can probably guess, the congregation felt free to dress in like manner. In this warm climate, many of them wore shorts, and there were lots of T-shirts as well (this included men and women). Anything went, and this carried over to body-piercings, tattoos, and pretty radical hairstyles. I can't remember ever seeing a person wear a suit in this church, and we attended there for over two years.

A couple of years earlier, I had served on staff at another church that was only three miles away from the highly casual church just mentioned. In this church, the pastor wore a gray, floor-length, formal preaching robe. If you have never seen one of these, just imagine a judge's robe. It had academic stripes on the arms that showed that the pastor had a doctoral degree. He also wore the academic hood (a colorful collar that hung around his neck and flowed down his back). His appearance made people in suits look casual!

No signs anywhere on the church grounds listed any particular dress code, but let me tell you, nobody wore shorts! There were lots of dark suits, and almost all of the women wore very nice dresses. I have no doubt that anyone wandering in from the "casual" church three miles away would have felt somewhat out of place. I am also confident that they would have been warmly welcomed. I mean it! These were gracious people that would have been glad to welcome someone dressed very casually. But I don't think someone who just came from the beach would have felt like they belonged in this church.

Most churches land somewhere in between these two churches when it comes to style. But the way we dress matters to most of us. Several years ago, when we were newly married, I learned this lesson. We were going out on a date with another couple. Sherry asked me to do something I had never thought to do before. She asked me to find out what the dress code would be for our dinner! It seemed like a strange question to a young Californian guy who did not own a tie. At that time, I was fashion challenged (and some people say I still am). But I asked, got the info, and passed it on. Lo and behold, when we met the other couple at the restaurant, everyone was dressed in a similar manner.

Our dinner would have tasted just as good, and we would have had just as nice a time if we had not talked about the dress code for the evening. But for me, this was one of my first lessons that clothing style is an important issue for lots of people. It is worth considering.

Action You Can Take

A Personal Style Evaluation

Take time to do the Personal Style Evaluation on the next page. If you have a number of family members attending church together, it would be helpful to list everyone's preference on the same graph. You might get a group picture that affirms what you already suspect or one that surprises you. As you seek to find a church you can really love, be sure to take everyone into account!

A Church Style Evaluation

After you have visited a church, take time to do the Church Style Evaluation on page 97. Be sure that everyone who attended with you gets a chance to answer. You might be surprised at the various perspectives you have on the same church experience.

Personal Style Evaluation

Mark where you see yourself on each graph below.

What kind of worship service style most helps me meet God and exalt his name?

Highly structured, liturgical, and clearly planned | Blended style | Very casual and free flowing. Surprise me!

What kind of musical style ushers me into a place of worship most naturally?

Classical, organ-led, hymn-based traditional music | Blended style (praise music and hymns with various instruments) | Highly contemporary, let-it-rock music

How outwardly expressive am I during worship in a church setting?

I don't feel comfortable showing outward expressions of worship | I am comfortable showing some outward expressions in worship | I am highly expressive in worship

What kind of dress helps me feel comfortable and ready to worship?

Very formal | Semiformal | Very casual

CHURCH STYLE EVALUATION

Mark where you see the church you visited on each graph below.

How would you describe the worship service?

Highly structured, liturgical, and clearly planned

Blended style

Very casual and free flowing

How would you describe the musical style of the service?

Classical, organ-led, hymn-based traditional music

Blended style (praise music and hymns with various instruments)

Highly contemporary, let-it-rock music

How outwardly expressive were the people in the church?

Not very comfortable showing outward expressions of worship

Somewhat comfortable showing outward expressions in worship

Highly expressive in worship

How would you describe the unwritten dress code at the church?

Very formal

Semiformal

Very casual

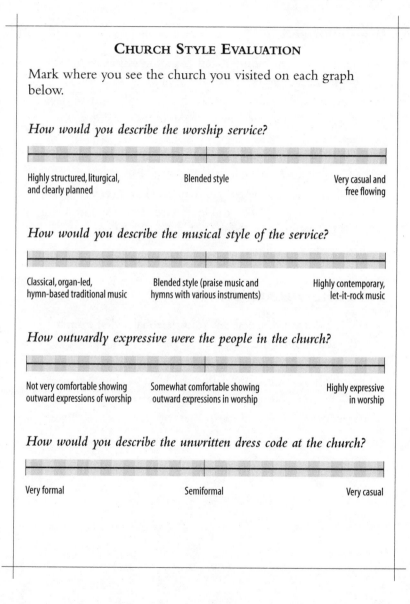

Prayer Direction

- Thank God for calling together groups of believers to begin local congregations with styles that are very different than your style. Pray that you will grow to have a greater appreciation for other styles of worship as the years pass.
- Ask God to give you growing freedom in how you express yourself in worship. Remember that in 2 Chronicles 20 the people responded in diverse ways, but *everybody responded* to God's work. Pray for a growing level of responsiveness to God's presence when you gather for worship.

For Further Reflection

- What did you learn about your personal style through the self-evaluation?
- What insights have you gained from your personal evaluation results concerning the kind of church that might help you meet with God and worship him with freedom?

Chapter 8

Sheep Stealing

THE SCENE IS ALL TOO FAMILIAR. We have all watched it happen on far too many occasions.

A pastor from a neighboring church is lurking in the parking lot of another church at the conclusion of a worship service. Waiting. Scheming. Plotting. Planning. With malicious intent, he creeps up on an unsuspecting member of the church flock. Closer and closer he moves like a lion ready to pounce on his prey. Finally, with lightening quickness he grabs a church member, ties him up, and shoves him in the back seat of his minivan. With the sound of tires screeching and the smell of rubber in the air, you realize it has happened again. Without any warning, another sheep has been stolen.

In less dramatic form, this familiar and painful scene happens week after week in the parking lots of churches all over the country. It is so common that the term *sheep stealing* has become part of the vocabulary of many believers. Sheep stealing is the practice of churches that increase their membership by luring and enticing people to leave their home congregation and go to a new church.

Throughout my years in ministry, I have heard pastors and church members mention their frustration over the practice of luring church members away. As a matter of fact, I've used the term sheep stealing on a few occasions myself. Many Christians become angry at those pastors and churches who are taking away their church members. But as I have thought about this topic over the years, something has troubled me and has caused me to become uncomfortable with this term. I have begun to question what lies behind the accusations and finger pointing.

I have come to the conclusion that, for the most part, sheep stealing is a dishonest term. Sheep are almost never stolen. Rarely is a happy church member lured away by another congregation. While pastors and church members cry over stolen sheep, they are missing the real tragedy. *In most cases, sheep are not stolen; they choose to leave.*

Why People Leave a Church

Some people are in the process of finding a church because they are seeking spiritual answers to life's questions and have never been part of the church before. They sense they will find answers to their questions in the church, and they are right! Others are in the process of finding a church because they have moved and know the importance of connecting with a new family of believers. There are also those who have been part of a congregation for years but have begun to feel the need to find a new church home. These people rarely leave their church home because they are lured away by another congregation in their community. In most cases, they decide to leave for a specific reason. People choose to leave a church for a number of reasons.

Many sheep leave *because they have grown hungry*. Let's face it; sheep tend to move to where they can graze and feed. When a church is not preaching the Word of God and is not feeding the members of the congregation with heavenly food, they tend to wander away. Also, when the Word is preached in a way that is boring or irrelevant, it doesn't nurture and feed the souls of those who listen. When there is a famine in the land, sheep will often migrate to greener pastures.

Some sheep leave *because they have been neglected*. When sheep are not cared for by a concerned shepherd, they often begin to wander. In the case of the church, the shepherd does not necessarily need to be ordained clergy, but whether clergy or laypeople, there must be people who care for and pastor church members. This enfolding ministry in the church is something that every person needs to experience, and extend. When church members have a sense that no one is available to help them in a time of need, they start looking for a flock where they will be cared for.

Other sheep begin to wander *because they have been used and abused*. There are too many people who leave their church because they are hurt, angry, and burned out. They have been asked to do far too much. They have been placed in areas of service and ministry with no concern for their giftedness or sense of call. And they have received little support, training, or encouragement along the way. Countless people have moved on from a church because they needed time to heal from an illness we call burnout. When the purposes of a church are not clear, it can become an unhealthy and hurtful place. People leave because the church is not functioning as the loving and life-giving body God intends it to be.

Yet other sheep leave *because of a change in church size.* Again, the size of a church is not a matter of core beliefs or a church's purpose, but some people prefer a certain size church. We had one family move to a smaller church when our church grew to over five hundred worshipers on a Sunday morning. One of the family members had some anxieties related to large groups and crowded places. Now that they are in a small church, this person is free to worship and be part of the body again. When we grew from five hundred to over a thousand, other members had to deal with the issue of being part of a rapidly growing church. Most who struggled with this have learned to find community in small groups and on service teams, but some still struggle with the size of the church. Those who see this as an important issue need to decide how important it is to them. If the shift in size stands in the way of their growing in faith and being freed to worship God, they might end up looking for a new church home.

Don't Take Changing Churches Lightly

When Steve and Helen and their two daughters came to visit our church for the first time, they were cautious. They were part of another local congregation but were considering looking for a new church home. They loved the church they were attending at the time. It was a church that had solid biblical beliefs. The big issue was their two girls. Over the years, many of the families with children the age of their girls had moved away, and Steve and

Helen felt it was time to look for a church with programs that would facilitate the girls' growth.

Steve and Helen were quite active in the church. They loved the people in their church. They felt no bitterness. But they did feel it was time to consider moving to a new church home. With a lot of prayer, some sadness, and a great deal of maturity, they decided to visit a few other churches and see if maybe there was one that would provide a spiritual community where their whole family, including their children, could grow in faith and connect in fellowship.

After coming to Corinth for a few weeks, and having decided that this church could be a place where they and their daughters could grow, they met with me so they could get a pastor's perspective. We had a wonderful conversation. I'll never forget when Helen said, "We don't want to be seen as one of those families that jump from place to place with no roots." I asked them, "How long have you been at your church?" They said, "For over fourteen years!" I assured them that no one would see them as uncommitted and flaky. After more time of prayer, they decided to make the move.

In the years that followed, Steve and Helen became part of our worship ministry. Both of their daughters grew in faith in beautiful ways and became part of our youth ministry. One of their girls later came on the church staff to lead a children's choir. We see this couple as a great example of a family who took the process of finding a new church home seriously and found joy in the journey.

Steve and Helen still love the people from their previous church and are glad when they see them. The whole family looks back on the years they spent at that church with joy and thankfulness. They pray for God's blessings on that congregation, and they praise God for the way he worked in their lives during their years of being part of that church family. When they knew it was time to make a move, they did so with the sensitivity and care you would expect from a follower of Christ. This made the process redemptive for the church they were leaving and a blessing for their family.

With Steve and Helen, the search for a new church came when they felt a need for spiritual growth opportunities and relational connections for their girls. Sometimes a family might consider a change in churches because of specific needs for the family's spiritual growth. For example, one family began coming to our church because we have a ministry to the deaf community. We have someone sign at two services each Sunday. This family's son is hearing impaired, and the whole family moved to Corinth Church so that he can develop his ability to sign and connect with others who are hearing impaired. It was a joy to watch this couple and their son find their place in our church and forge a special relationship with the growing number of people who sing with their hands, listen with their eyes, and praise God with full hearts!

If you are considering leaving your church, it is very important to spend time in prayer before making a decision. Don't leave a church for any reason until you have prayed and asked for God's leading. Leaving a church should never be a casual or hasty decision. Prayer on your own and with trusted Christian friends should always be part of the process. If you pray and feel you should stay where you are, stay! This probably means God has plans for you where you are, even if you have some struggles there. Following God's will and plan for you always comes first!

Don't Leave!

There are times when you should be cautious about leaving a church. We have identified three unhealthy reasons some people will leave a church. First, *don't leave a church because you are feeling convicted of the truth and it makes you uncomfortable*. Sometimes a sermon or a Sunday school lesson cuts to a person's heart. The Holy Spirit is bringing conviction, and they feel uneasy. Maybe a pastor preaches about generosity in giving, and they don't want to give; they are battling selfishness. Perhaps a small group is studying moral purity, and someone is uncomfortable because they are crossing biblical boundaries in a relationship. Maybe a Sunday school leader is teaching on integrity and honesty in the workplace, and someone becomes angry because they are breaking all kinds of rules at their job. These are not reasons to leave a church; they are good reasons to stay! Don't go looking for a church that tries to lower biblical standards just to make people feel comfortable.

A second caution is *don't leave a church because you have been caught in a sin*. Many people make a poor choice and get caught. The natural response is to run away and find a church where they can start fresh and no one knows about their sin. Yet God often wants a person in this situation to stay right where they are and let their church family love them and help them through this difficult time. The community of faith can keep them accountable, ask tough questions, and pray for them. This can often be a reason to stay and connect even more closely to the church. Sadly, those whose sin becomes public often run away as fast as they can. This is a mistake.

A third caution is *don't leave a church because you have had a conflict with someone.* Too often when tensions have flared, words have been exchanged, and feelings have been hurt, people want to avoid the difficult process of reconciliation, so they think about leaving. They might say to themselves something like, "Well, if that is the way people in this church are going to behave, I'll find a church where people are kinder." We don't ever want to minimize a person's pain over a broken relationship, but the Bible has a great deal to say about how we need to seek healing when we walk through times of relational conflict. Often the wisest choice is to stay and work through a process of relational healing. A person who leaves a church for this reason just might find they have to leave a whole series of churches. Because the church is people, we are all bound to hit some bumpy relational roads through the years. The question is, How will we respond?

Over the years we have seen that those who wander from church to church for no particular reason tend to remain sad and unsatisfied. These sheep wander from pasture to pasture, always thinking the grass will be greener on the other side of the fence. When they get to a new church, these "church shoppers and hoppers" can't seem to fit in. They are able to find something wrong everywhere they go. At some point, those who can never find a church they can love might want to stop and recognize that the one common factor in all of these situations is them! Maybe they need to do a heart check and make sure they are not coming in with the wrong attitudes and unrealistic expectations.

Prayer Direction

- Pray that the church, all over the world, will stay committed to the teachings of the Bible! Pray that the beliefs of the church will stay pure.
- If you are in the process of looking for a church home because you are considering leaving the church you are presently attending, and God convicts you that you are leaving with wrong motives, pray about staying and seeking restored relationship with God's people in your present congregation.

For Further Reflection

- What changes or compromises in core beliefs would cause you to leave a church?
- What dramatic style shifts might cause you to think about looking for a new church home?

Action You Can Take

Ideas to Help You Leave Well

No matter why you leave a church, certain things will make your departure healthy and life-giving. If you are leaving your church, these four ideas might help you walk through the process with a sense of health and peace.

Connect with the pastor or a church leader. If you know it is time to find a new church home, be sure to meet with the pastor or a church leader. Because you are part of a spiritual family, a face-to-face contact is very important. In this meeting, it would be helpful to communicate four things:

- *Give words of blessing.* Express how you have been helped in your spiritual life through being part of this fellowship of believers. Be specific and give as much affirmation and encouragement as possible.
- *Express concerns honestly.* If you have concerns about something in the life of the church, talk about them. In Ephesians 4:15 we are taught to speak the truth, but to do so in a loving way. Very specifically, if there is a concern that has caused you to feel you need to find a new church home, the leadership of your present church will want to know.
- *Give suggestions for positive change.* If you are leaving due to a specific concern, and if you have lovingly expressed that concern, be ready to suggest how you believe the church might change to avoid having others leave for the same reasons.
- *Commit to pray faithfully for the church and the church leaders.* Let the pastor or leader know that you want God's best for the church and that you will be praying for God's hand to be upon the church.

Some people leaving a church will have only positive affirmations to communicate. Others might have some concerns to share. In any case, a face-to-face contact before leaving can be helpful both for the person leaving and for the church.

Chapter 9

Serious Business

SOME YEARS AGO we met a couple that was in the process of finding a new church home. They were going to look for a house in the greater Grand Rapids area. But what was unique about this couple was that they went about this in a way that would seem backward to many people.

Due to a work-related move, this couple was settling in our community. They had to uproot and find a new home and a new church. Most people shop for a house first and then try to find a church near their new home. But this couple did it the other way around. They were spending time visiting churches and praying about where they would set down spiritual roots. Once they found their church home, then they went looking for a house near their new church. Wow! Talk about being committed to finding a church you can love! This couple made it a priority in their lives.

Would You Buy a House on a Whim?

Finding the right church could be compared to the process of finding a new house. No one would just walk up

109

to the first house with a For Sale sign and buy it. Anyone looking for a new house would first gather good information about the community by going to a realtor, a web site, or other up-to-date information sources and form a list of houses that seem like valid options. They would then walk through some of these homes and try to discover which ones seemed best. Finally, they would narrow it down to one house. This process parallels the church-search process we will be presenting in this chapter.

Step 1: Looking at the Landscape and Gathering Options

God can lead a person to a church in a multitude of ways. There is no perfect process for finding a church. But there are some helpful guidelines, and these are what we will be looking at in this section. Begin your process by gathering a list of churches that seem like valid options. At this point, don't worry about all the details about the church; just begin gathering church names. Here are some possible sources to draw from:

- Churches near where you live.
- Churches you have heard mentioned by others who really love them.
- If you have a denominational background and preference, check with your regional denominational leaders.
- Do an Internet search.
- Look through the yellow pages.
- Ask friends or work associates in the area if they know of good churches in the area.

- Check with the local chamber of commerce or call the city for a listing of churches.

The goal in this part of the process is not finding the right church; it is simply gathering a list of potential churches. Once you have some church names that seem like possible options, you are ready to move on to step 2.

Step 2: Getting Basic Information and Narrowing the Field

Once you have a list of possible churches, the fun begins. Now you can make some contacts with these churches and learn a little more about them. We would suggest that you *not* start visiting churches until you have done a brief interview with a church leader. There are three main ways this can be done. You can make a phone call and speak with someone from the church staff. We would suggest you ask for ten minutes at the most. Another option is to send an e-mail with specific questions and ask a member of the church staff or a member of the church board to respond to your questions. The third option is to drop into the church office and have a brief conversation with a church leader. In some cases, you might get a response from a pastor, but this is not necessary. Also, many churches have excellent web sites. Be sure to use this source of information as you are learning about a church. The key is to get your questions answered by someone who knows the church well. As a matter of fact, if you have a friend who attends one of the churches on your list, you can interview them.

After you have spoken to someone from each church, you will have a fairly good sense of which churches might be a good fit for you. We would suggest you narrow it down to two or three that seem to connect for you. Once you do this, you are ready to move to step 3.

Step 3: The First Visit

Over the coming weeks, enjoy the process of visiting a few churches. Pray that your heart will be open to worship. Ask God to help you connect with people in each congregation and to grow in your appreciation of Christians from various churches. This might be the first time you have visited different groups of believers, and there is a great chance it will be an enjoyable experience. Appreciate the differences of each church and celebrate the common expressions of worship and praise. Here are a few suggestions that may help you as you visit each church.

Pray before you go. Be sure to bathe the whole process in prayer. Ask the Lord to bless your visit. Invite the Holy Spirit to give you wisdom and insight. Put the whole process in God's hands; he cares about this even more than you do! You might want to look back at chapter 4 for ideas.

Allow plenty of time for your visit. Don't just pop in at the last minute and run off immediately after the service. Show up fifteen minutes early. Wander around. Pick up some literature. Meet a few people. If the church has an education program, plan to be part of it. If you attend as a family, have your children attend classes or youth gatherings that are held in tandem with the worship service. If you have an infant, look over the nursery and ask questions. When the service and classes are over, linger a little longer. Allow time to look, listen, and learn about this community of believers.

Meet people halfway. Step out and greet people. It is fine to wait and see if people reach out to you and greet you, but it is also appropriate for you to greet people and introduce yourself. Feel free to extend a hand and say, "Hello, I'm visiting your church for the first time!" This might just spark a conversation that will be the beginning of a friendship.

Look for an information area. Often churches have designated people to help answer questions for you. If the church you are visiting has people in this role, they will be thrilled to meet you. Feel free to ask questions, to ask for a little tour of the facility, or just to chat.

Have a positive attitude. Every time you gather with God's people to worship, learn, and share in fellowship, you can expect God to be present. Gathering with God's people is a joy and a privilege. Be ready for good things to happen.

Reflect and evaluate. After your visit, take time to pray and to reflect on your experience. The material at the end of chapters 5 through 8 will help you in this process. The resources at the end of this chapter will also help give you direction.

Once you have visited each church, take time to pray about which one seemed to be the best fit for you. If you are in this process as a couple or as a family, spend time talking and praying together. At this point, you are ready to do one of two things. If one of the churches you visited seems like a strong possibility, you are ready to move to step 4. If none of the churches seems to fit, go back to step 1 in this process and start over again.

Step 4: Committing One Month

If you think you might have found the right church, commit to one full month of worship at that church. Be consistent and do all you can to connect in the life of the church. Use some of the suggestions from step 3 to help you stay focused. We strongly suggest that you attend both the worship service and the education programs.

If you are looking for a church as a family, do all you can to help your children experience the full life of the church. It might be wise to talk with the leaders responsible for the areas of ministry where your children will be attending for the month. Let them know about the process you are in and invite them to pray for your whole family, and especially for your children. If you have a junior high student who is going to attend a youth event and doesn't know anyone, ask the leader if he or she will connect your child with another student who can introduce your child to the other kids. Most children's and youth leaders and volunteers are more than happy to help in this way.

Don't jump into anything, such as a small group, that demands a long-term commitment, but connect where you can. If the church has a midweek program for adults, teens, and children, make a commitment to attend this also. Do all you can to experience the life of the congregation.

During this month, be open to meeting people, starting friendships, and asking good questions. It is a time to explore and learn about the church. Go deeper with your questions about beliefs, purpose, and style. Don't be shy about learning more about the church. It is better to learn all you can up front than have lots of surprises down the road. Enjoy this time of worship, growth, and connecting with God's people. And each step of the way, pray that God will lead you.

Step 5: Making a Decision

After a month of consistent relationship with this community of believers, you will have a pretty good sense of their core beliefs, purpose, and style of worship. You will also have gotten to know some people. At this point you can make an informed and prayerful decision whether this is a church you can really love.

Ask yourself if you are confident that this is a church that will help you grow deeper as a follower of Christ. If you have prayed and reflected along the way and feel God has led you to this church, you are ready to begin moving into the life of this congregation. We will look at this in chapter 11. If you believe this is not the right church for you, begin again at step 1 or 2. Don't look at this time as wasted. Know that God has been leading you each step of the way and that he will lead you to a church you can love. When Israel was in a difficult and dark time of their history, God spoke these words to his people: "'For I know the plans I have for you,' declares the LORD, 'plans to prosper you and not to harm you, plans to give you hope and a future'" (Jer. 29:11).

Prayer Direction

- Commit to pray for each church you contact and each one you visit. Use this season of your life as a time to lift up various churches in your community in a way you may never have done before.
- Ask God to give you warmth and boldness as you visit churches.

Action You Can Take

Asking the Right Questions

Take time to call a church and do the interview on the next page.

SAMPLE INTERVIEW SHEET

(FOR A PHONE CONVERSATION OR A FACE-TO-FACE VISIT)

Ask only two or three questions from each section below. Don't feel you have to ask all the questions. Also, feel free to write one or two questions of your own.

Introduction

Hello, my name is _____. I am looking for a church home in the area and am wondering if there is someone who knows your church fairly well that I could speak with for about ten minutes?

Basic Information

☐ When are your worship services?

☐ Could you tell me about your education program?

☐ How might an adult (teen, child) connect in the life of your church?

☐ How many worshipers attend on a normal weekend?

☐ Do you have a denominational affiliation, and if you do, how does this relationship impact your church?

☐

☐

Questions about Beliefs

☐ What does your church believe about the Bible?

☐ What do you believe about Jesus Christ?

☐ What do you believe about the Trinity?

☐ How do you believe a person comes to salvation and a relationship with God?

☐ Do you have a printed statement of faith or beliefs that you could mail to me?

☐ (Add any questions you might have about specific beliefs you want to know about.)

☐

☐

Questions about Purpose

☐ What is the role of worship in the life of your church?

☐ What does your church do to help people feel connected and part of the congregation?

☐ If I wanted to get involved in an area of service in your church, what programs do you have to help me discover my God-given abilities and my place in ministry?

☐ How does your church help each of its members keep growing deeper in faith and more mature as a Christian?

☐ How does your church reach out to the community and share Jesus' love with others?

☐ Do you have a church purpose statement I could look at?

☐
☐

Questions about Style

☐ How would you describe the style of music in your worship services?

☐ How do most of the men and women dress when they come to the main worship service at your church?

☐ Some services are very formal and others are informal; how would you describe yours?

☐ If you have a printed order of worship, could I get a copy from the last two weeks?

☐
☐

General Questions

☐ What is one thing you love about your church?

☐ What draws people to your church and keeps them there?

☐ Is there anything else you would like to tell me about your church?

☐
☐

Thank you so much for your time! I would ask you to pray for me (and my family, if it applies) as I look for the right church.

PART 3

Finding Your Place among God's People

A Healthy Body

OVER TWENTY YEARS AGO, we heard people talking about the impact that TV would have on worship attendance in the local church. As some pastors started televising their Sunday services, we heard people say things like, "No one is going to drive to a church service when they can just watch a service on TV." Others made comments about how these powerful TV preachers would empty the pews of local churches because people would stay home and watch them rather than go to a church with a preacher who could not communicate with the same oratory flair.

Yet as the years passed, people kept making it a priority to get in their cars and drive to their local church. Rather than draining local congregations, TV preachers helped people understand who Jesus is, and many viewers came to a genuine saving faith. Many of these people then went out and started looking for a local church to attend.

With the advent of the Internet, we again heard talk of the devastating impact this would have on local congregations.

Futurists wrote of "virtual churches" that would replace local congregations. The "prophetic" word was that people would get their spiritual needs met through services on the Internet, religious chat rooms, and e-communities of faith. Years later, as far as we can tell, this has not materialized. People are drawing from excellent resources on the Internet to strengthen their spiritual lives, but the local church continues to draw people from every walk of life.

What is it about the local church that has such power and force? Why did Jesus say, "I will build my church, and the gates of Hades will not overcome it" (Matt. 16:18)? Why do tens of thousands of people start the process of looking for a church every year? We believe it is because there is a level of fellowship, community, and intimacy in the church that can't be experienced anywhere else. In a way, the community of the church is a foretaste of heaven. In the church, we find a level of connection that satisfies something deep in our souls.

Belonging to a Fellowship

In J. R. R. Tolkien's trilogy, the *Lord of the Rings,* there is a decisive moment when a group of very diverse characters are forged into a fellowship. This fellowship is made up of an unlikely cast: four hobbits, two men, an elf, a dwarf, and a wizard. These nine beings become the fellowship of the ring. They have a common goal and begin to strive toward it with great purpose and passion. Each one is needed and brings unique abilities and insight to the fellowship. As a group, they accomplish far more than any of them could have on their own.

Throughout history, many people have referred to the church as a fellowship. When we are part of a local congregation, we discover that while all the members of the church might be quite different, they make up one unit. Each person has something to offer, and their contribution makes the church stronger than it would be without them. Members of a local church function with a common sense of purpose and direction. Each member is needed. A local church can accomplish so much more than a disconnected group of Christians. The Bible uses a helpful and tangible illustration to make this crystal clear.

The Church Is like a Physical Body

Throughout the New Testament, the church is compared to a body. Think about how much sense this makes. A physical body has many and various parts, but together they form one unit. Each part has a different function, but all are needed. No person would ever willingly give up a foot, an arm, or an eye. If one of these parts is lost, the whole body is impacted. Every part of the body is important and needed, and offers a valuable contribution. I don't know all the scientific explanations of how my liver works and all that it does to keep me healthy. What I do know is that I have visited people in the hospital who have had something go wrong with their liver. Believe me, a healthy liver is essential for the health of the body! Every part of the body is needed, even if we don't know exactly how it fits into the big picture. The apostle Paul put it this way:

Now the body is not made up of one part but of many. If the foot should say, "Because I am not a hand, I do not belong to the body," it would not for that reason cease to be part of the body. And if the ear should say, "Because I am not an eye, I do not belong to the body," it would not for that reason cease to be part of the body. If the whole body were an eye, where would the sense of hearing be? If the whole body were an ear, where would the sense of smell be? But in fact God has arranged the parts in the body, every one of them, just as he wanted them to be. If they were all one part, where would the body be? As it is, there are many parts, but one body.

The eye cannot say to the hand, "I don't need you!" And the head cannot say to the feet, "I don't need you!" . . . there should be no division in the body, but that its parts should have equal concern for each other.

—1 Corinthians 12:14–21, 25

Just like the parts of a physical body, followers of Christ are connected to each other. In a local congregation, each person has a part to play, a function to perform, a gift to use. No one can say that another person is not needed in the church. And no one ought to ever say, "I am not needed." God makes it clear that each person who follows Jesus is needed in the fellowship of the church. You might be a hand, a foot, an eye, or a liver. You could be called to play the role of a hobbit, an elf, or a dwarf. Whatever your role, it was given to you by God, and you are needed, valuable, and critical for the health of Christ's body, the church.

Have you ever been trying to drive a nail into a board and missed? Do you remember what it felt like when the head of the hammer missed the nail and hit your thumb? When you think of it, can you still feel how the pain of that blow (on one small part of your body) ran from the tips of your toes to the top of your head? We all know that feeling and understand how the body is connected when it comes to pain. In a similar way, we all know the feeling of the first bite of a food we love. The moment we taste imported chocolate, fresh salsa, homemade cookies right out of the oven, or our favorite fruit, our whole body enjoys it! Our taste buds might get the first moment of enjoyment, but it seems like our whole body joins in and tingles with delight. In the New Testament, we learn that the members of God's spiritual body also live with this kind of mutual satisfaction and pain.

> There should be no division in the body, but that its parts should have equal concern for each other. If one part suffers, every part suffers with it; if one part is honored, every part rejoices with it.
> —1 Corinthians 12:25–26

The Head of the Body Is Jesus

If the church is a body, who is the head? Who directs the body and helps all the parts to function together? Who gives ultimate leadership? The answer is Jesus! "And he [Jesus] is the head of the body, the church" (Col. 1:18). When a church struggles and becomes a place of conflict rather than peace, it is often because Jesus is not being invited to be the head of the body. Some church bodies become unhealthy when the primary leadership is given to the pastor, the church board, long-term members who believe the church is "theirs," or even to the people who give the biggest checks in the offering plate. The moment any person or group of people takes over the place of headship, the church is in danger. Only Jesus can be the head of his body, the church. When Jesus is in the ultimate place of leadership, he will call the right people to serve as pastors, board members, and leaders of the many different ministries in the church.

Jesus Calls Us into Community

Sherry and I spent the first ten years of our relationship in southern California, where I grew up. We were always in close driving distance to the beach. During the decade we attended a local church in California, we heard people say things like, "I don't need to go to some church building to experience God's presence! I just take walks along the beach and experience God there." What they were saying is that their personal connection with God was enough.

I believe people can meet with God while walking along the Pacific Ocean. As a matter of fact, some of my most intimate times with God have been at Huntington Beach, Newport Beach, and on the tip of the Balboa Peninsula at a place called the Wedge. I love meeting God in creation and still find the smell of salt water and the crashing of waves very worshipful!

When we moved to Michigan, we heard the same sort of story. People in this part of the country talk about not needing "church" because they meet God on the shores of the Great Lakes or in the woods. Sherry would tell you that few things stir her heart to praise and help her feel intimate with her Creator more than a sunset on Lake Michigan.

The question is, should these experiences take the place of being part of a local church? Are they enough?

Jesus' answer is clear. He calls us into community and fellowship with each other in a way that blesses us and shows the world he is alive! The way we love each other is the greatest sign of his power and presence to a world that looks on and wonders if there is anything to the Christian faith. Jesus said, "A new command I give you: Love one another. As I have loved you, so you must love one another. By this all men will know that you are my disciples, if you love one another" (John 13:34–35). For the sake of God's plan, the church, and the world, it is time for us to see just how important it is for us to be part of a local body of believers.

We Need the Church, and the Church Needs Us!

One day while shopping, we saw a perfect example of how the body of Christ is made up of many parts that make a whole. We saw two men coming out of a store. One was paralyzed and in a wheelchair. From what we could tell, the man seemed to be a quadriplegic. His friend was pushing him and functioning as his legs and arms on their shopping trip. What caught our attention was the fact that the gentleman in the wheelchair was giving his friend the directions he needed to steer the chair correctly. He was doing this because the man pushing the chair was blind. He could not have done his part if his friend did not have eyes to see where they were going. Each one of these men would have had a very hard time on a shopping trip if he were alone. Together they made their way from store to store with relative ease and obvious joy.

We were so impacted by the way these two men added to each other's lives that we talked about it a long time that day and have spoken of it many times since. We both commented about how this has become a picture of the body of Christ in our minds. In the church we learn that we need each other! We don't have all the abilities and skills needed to move through life in a healthy way. But when we are connected with the other members of Christ's body, we can become all God wants us to be.

Some people say, "The church doesn't need me. I'm not important. I will never be missed. I don't want to be part of a local congregation." If this is you, you need to know that you are needed. You do matter. You are missed. The church will be stronger and healthier if you find your place and become an active part of the body of Christ.

Each part of the body is needed, and the whole body suffers if some of the parts are not functioning. Sherry learned this in a personal way when her grandmother had a stroke. Her family's story might be similar to your own.

My grandma lived only a short distance from my home when I was growing up. It was not unusual for me to visit her and my grandpa three or four times a week. When I walked in my grandma's home, I always found the same picture. I would find her in the kitchen baking apple pie, chocolate-chip cookies, her famous Christmas peanut brittle, or some other delicacy she wanted to share with family and friends. She moved about her kitchen with great ease, and we could always tell she was joyful to be doing something she loved. She was like an artist. The kitchen was her studio where she used sugar, flour, and chocolate to make her masterpieces.

One day this creative process came to an abrupt stop. Grandma and the rest of family knew things would be different from that day on. In one moment everything changed. My grandma suffered a stroke that left one side of her body paralyzed. Even though half of her body still moved and functioned as before, the impact of the nonfunctioning parts affected the movement of her entire body. For the remaining eleven years of her life she never moved around that kitchen in the way I had enjoyed watching for so many years. My grandmother lost movement in only part of her body, but it affected everything.

When we declare that we are not needed in the church, we are missing the clear message God is sending us. We are needed. We are valuable. We have something to offer that will bring health, vitality, and life to the body of Christ.

It is a joy to realize that we belong to the body of Christ, his church. We are needed. Just as there are many parts in a physical body and all of them are valued, so in the church, every person matters. The reason TV worship services and religious chat rooms on the Internet have not replaced, and never will replace, the local church is that they do not give people a place to connect as the body of Christ. We need to be together; we need each other. And Jesus rejoices in us, his body, the church.

Prayer Direction

- Ask God to help you see the unique abilities and gifts he has given to you and how you can use these gifts to bring strength to his body.
- Invite God to begin preparing you to be an active member as you look for a church you can really love. Ask God to make you ready to be connected in some area of ministry that fits the unique gifts he has given you.

For Further Reflection

- Once I am part of a church, what are some of the abilities, talents, and gifts I have that could benefit and build up the church and make it healthier?
- What is one step I can take as I connect in a local church?

Action You Can Take

Bible Study

Take time in the coming days to study the following Bible passages and use the questions provided for personal reflection or discussion with others.

Read the following passages from the Bible:

- 1 Corinthians 12:12–26
- Ephesians 4:11–16

Reflect on or discuss the following questions:

- In light of these two passages, what is God's vision for how his people connect with each other?
- What are some of the benefits when God's people function together like a healthy body? What are some of the consequences if we don't?

Connecting in the Life of the Church

IN CHAPTER 9, we looked at how finding a church home can be compared to finding a new house. We looked at the process of gathering a list of many options, narrowing the field, visiting some of the options, and then making a choice. When you are buying a new home, there is a point when you say, "This is the one!" At that point, you move forward with making it official. Then, when all the papers are signed and everything is in order, you get the thrill of actually moving into your new home.

This chapter focuses on the process of moving into a new church home. There are a number of things you can do that will make the process go smoothly and make it rich and exciting. There are also some things you might want to avoid. Between the two of us we have been in the church for over six decades. Our hope is that we can point out some of the pitfalls to avoid and the steps to be enjoyed along the way.

At this point, you have visited the church for a number of Sundays, but you have been looking at it as one church among various options. Now you are looking at it as your church home. Before you were connected, but now you are committed. So far you have been learning about the church, now you are becoming part of the body of believers. It is time to move into your new church home!

Things to Do As You Move into Your Church Home

Make regular attendance a priority. The habits and patterns you set in the first few months of attending your new church will set the tone for the years ahead. Be sure you make regular attendance a priority in your heart and your schedule. As much as possible, be with God's people in worship each week. Also, if you decide to be part of a small group or a weekly class, be committed to attending each time they meet.

All of us have times we will have to miss church or a gathering with God's people, and some people have work that takes them away on occasion or even regularly. But it is important to be with God's people when you can and to pray for them when you are absent. Our attitude toward worship and gathering with the family of God should mirror the heart of the psalmist:

> I rejoiced with those who said to me,
> "Let us go to the house of the LORD."
> —Psalm 122:1

We need to hear the words of exhortation that were given to those who were part of the early church:

> Let us not give up meeting together, as some are in the habit of doing, but let us encourage one another—and all the more as you see the Day approaching.
>
> —Hebrews 10:25

One of the best things you can do as you enter the life of a local church is simply to be there! Everything else can grow with time. Nothing will grow out of choosing a new church home if you are never there. Make regular attendance part of your lifestyle.

Pray for God's help and guidance. As we have said over and over, prayer should be part of every aspect of your church-search process. As you begin to settle into your new church home, be deeply prayerful on many levels. Pray that your heart will be open and responsive to what God wants to do in you and through you as you become part of this church family. Pray that your new church will experience God's power and presence each time they gather. If you are attending as a couple or as a family, pray that each family member will find a place to connect in fellowship and service.

Be sensitive to the whole family. If you are attending as a family, be sensitive to each person. Sometimes a whole family will be excited and passionate about a church, but one member of the family is having a harder time connecting and feeling that they belong in this group of people. Do all you can to help each person in the family find a place of belonging.

Connect in smaller gatherings. Whether a church has a hundred people or many thousands, we still need to relate to each other in smaller groups. This can happen in Sunday school classes, youth groups, small groups, service teams, or other settings. The key is for each of us to be in a setting where we know people by name and they know us. If we just attend a worship service and blend in, we miss the joy of intimate community that God wants us to have with his people. The best time to begin connecting in a small group or class is when you first start moving into the life of the church. This will help you begin forging friendships, and it will make a church of any size feel more like a family.

Many people have the misconception that small churches are warm and intimate and large churches are cold and impersonal. We have learned that this is simply not the case. Very small churches can be cold and unfriendly, and large churches can be open-armed and warm. The opposite can also be true. The key to feeling connected in a church of any size is being part of a small cluster of people where you can build friendships, accountability, and genuine community.

Find a small way to serve. We suggest that you not get overextended in serving as you begin to enter the life of your new church but instead find a small way to serve. Offer to be a greeter once a month, serve coffee occasionally, help as an usher, assist in the nursery, or perform some other small act of service. This will let you connect with people and start a habit of serving that will grow in the months to come. Start small and then see what doors God opens for ministry. If you aren't sure about where you will serve best over the long haul, be sure to take a class on spiritual gifts as soon as you can and begin praying for God to lead you to your place in long-term, gift-based ministry in the church.

Do your part to meet people and connect. Make it a point to meet someone new each week. If you see someone you haven't met, go out of your way to introduce yourself and say hello. When you do, let them know you are new in the church and are trying to get to know some people. You might even want to think about some questions beforehand that you can ask when you meet someone new. Here are a few ideas: How long have you been part of this church? What is one thing you love about this church? What brought you to this church, and what keeps you here? If you make a point of greeting people warmly, you will be amazed at how quickly you can find yourself feeling at home.

At our church, we often say that if a new person will come 10 percent of the way, we will come the other 90 percent. The fact is, some people enter new places easily and like the process of meeting new people. Others take a little longer to feel at home and find the process more difficult. No matter how you are wired, it is important to meet people and connect in your new church. Be careful that you don't take a posture of standing back and waiting for everyone else to come to you.

In one of the churches we have served, we had two interactions with families who came to the church with an unhealthy attitude. They stayed away from people and were cold to those who tried to connect with them. These people left after a short time, both families giving the same critique and evaluation: the church was not warm and accepting of them. They had wanted the church members to come 100 percent of the way to meet them and invite them in. And when these families pushed people away, they wanted the church members to keep trying.

If you come 50 percent of the way and meet people in the middle, you will find yourself warmly received. If you are a little shy but do your part to meet people 25 percent of the way, you will still find yourself with a growing number of relationships in a short time. What is important is that you do your part!

Bless and encourage. As you enter into the life of a new church, look for opportunities to bless what is good. Thank a Sunday school teacher for working with your child, send a note to a youth leader to let them know you appreciate their ministry, affirm a nursery helper for their willingness to miss worship and care for children, e-mail the pastor and share what you learned from a sermon, or thank the custodians for all they do behind the scenes to keep the facility up! There are countless ways you can extend encouragement. From the beginning of your relationship with your new church, be a source of blessing to others.

Be patient. The church is people, and it takes time to get to know people and find your place in the congregation. If you are coming from a church you attended for many years, don't expect the same level of intimacy right away. It might have taken years, or a lifetime, to develop the kind of closeness you had in your previous church. Be confident that God will develop the ties and relationships you long to have, but let him do it in his timing. Instant intimacy rarely lasts.

Begin the discipline of giving to support the work of the church. Being part of a church means supporting the ministry not only by serving and praying but also by giving. When a follower of Christ thinks about giving of their resources to God's work, two key words should come to mind: cheerful and generous. Read what the apostle Paul says about our practice of giving:

Remember this: Whoever sows sparingly will also reap sparingly, and whoever sows generously will also reap generously. Each man should give what he has decided in his heart to give, not reluctantly or under compulsion, for God loves a cheerful giver.

—2 Corinthians 9:6–7

Pray for a heart that finds joy in giving. Ask God to help you grow in generosity. Pray that you will joyfully do your part in supporting the ministry of your church.

Invite others to your new church. From the moment you move into your new church home, pray that you will be bold in inviting others to the church. If you had people praying for your church-search process and they don't have a church home, invite them to come to a worship service or to some kind of non-threatening event held at the church or sponsored by the church. It is never too early to begin reaching out to others and seeking to connect them with a spiritual community of people who will love them and tell them about God's love.

If you have ever moved into a new home or apartment, you know that it can be a lot of fun and a lot of work. The work and fun seem to go hand in hand. It takes a lot of energy and time to move all the furniture into a room, do some decorating, maybe paint or wallpaper, and get everything where you want it. But when you step back and look at the end result, you see that the work was worth it. Moving into a new church is similar. It is fun and exciting, but there is work involved. Enjoy the process, then step back, smile, and thank God for helping you each step of the way.

Things to Avoid As You Move into Your Church Home

Don't come in and try to take over. If you were extremely involved in a previous church, be careful not to come in and be overly aggressive. Remember that there are people in the church who have been faithfully serving there for a long time. Many of them have spent a lot of years and poured a lot of love into specific ministries in the church. If you have certain gifts and abilities, be willing to help. But as you enter the life of a church, be cautious about stepping in and being overassertive. Take a supporting role at first. Learn by watching. Get involved in training opportunities. Be ready to exercise the heart of a servant before you exercise the gifts of leadership. If you give the impression that you are coming in to take over and make things the way you think they should be, there is a good chance you will put off the very people you should be learning from.

There is another side to this coin, however. You might not have any desire to take over some area of the church ministry, but someone might come up to you and say, "I know just what you need! You need to lead our women's ministry." Or maybe someone learns you are a schoolteacher, and the second week you are at the church they say, "I think you should help lead our Sunday school program." We are not saying it's wrong to consider ministry opportunities that are offered to you. What we are saying is that you should become part of the life of the church and get to know its heartbeat and culture before you take on too much leadership.

Build relationships before taking on too much responsibility. Allow time for relationships to grow. Commit to knowing the church before you take on too much responsibility. For the first three to six months, invest a lot of time in getting to know people. Also, if you are attending as a family, invest in helping your children find their place in the church. Listen to them and learn about the church. Discover the joy of this new family of which you are now a part. If you meet some people you enjoy, invite them out for lunch or have them over for coffee. Make it a priority to invest your time in relationships first.

Avoid being critical and judgmental. There are no perfect churches. We will look at this reality in the next chapter. This means that you will see things in your church that you might not like. Be careful about being critical and judgmental of people, leaders, ministries, musicians, or other "easy targets" in the church. Everyone can find things to complain about and criticize, but God calls us to spend a lot more energy on building up and blessing.

This doesn't mean that real concerns should be ignored. But if you come across as a highly critical person, especially as you are first moving into a new church, you could brand yourself as a complainer. If you have a valid concern, prayerfully and humbly share it with the right person. Don't develop a pattern of critiquing and criticizing.

Don't expect your new church to be just like your old church. Be careful about attitudes you might carry with you from your last church. If you just loved your old church, take care not to make a lot of comparisons. You might be tempted to say things like, "I like it better the way we did it at our old church; what we did there was . . ." Be careful not to develop the unhealthy pattern of constantly telling people how great your old church was and how your new church doesn't measure up. Don't give people the sense that you want your new church to be transformed into a replica of your old church.

To be sure, there might be some great ideas you can bring from your old church that will translate easily to your new church and be a great help. But be careful not to push these ideas too hard, too often, or too early as you are starting your relationship with your new church. In these first few months, making lots of comparisons is probably a bad idea.

On the other end of the continuum, be careful not to make comparisons with your old church by telling people how bad it was compared to this church. This might seem flattering, but it isn't a healthy pattern to develop. Don't affirm the pastor by saying, "What a great sermon! My old pastor bored me to tears! I'm so glad I don't have to listen to him anymore." Comparisons that put your old church in a poor light should be avoided.

You are in a new season. Enjoy it. Don't forget your past, but don't let it rule your present.

Prayer Direction

- Ask God to help you find an opportunity to serve in some small way.
- Pray for a spirit that is eager to encourage and bless, not criticize.

For Further Reflection

- Do you tend to be an encourager or a critic by nature? What can you do to develop your ability to bless and build others up?
- Why is connecting in a small group or a class setting important as you become part of your new community of faith?

Action You Can Take

Write a Letter

Sit down this week and write a letter (or send an e-mail) to someone in the church who helped you in your process of finding a new church home. Maybe it was the person you interviewed when you first called the church. Maybe it was someone who reached out to you and made you feel welcome the first time you came to church. It might be someone who reached out to one of your children. Whoever it is, write a short note and let this person know how God used them in your process of finding a church home.

Chapter 12

Loving the Church You Have Found

SOME YEARS AGO, a new church was starting in our community. We began getting advertisements in our mailbox inviting us to visit this newly forming congregation. What surprised us was the tone and nature of the ads. The impressions and feeling these ads gave was: "Are you tired of churches that expect so much from you? Wouldn't you love to come to a church that gives you everything and asks for nothing back? Come to our new church and have all your needs met!"

We talked with a few friends who had received these promotional invitations to see if they were hearing the same message. They told us that they were. We were all troubled because we knew that a church built on the idea that people can come and get, get, get and never give back was profoundly unhealthy.

Imagine a friend saying to you, "Here's the deal. I want our relationship to be one-way. I am going to let you support me in times of need. I will tell you when I need a ride to the airport, and you can come drive me. If I'm low on cash, I will let you give me money. You can listen to me, care for me, and help me out whenever I need you. How does that sound?"

You listen to your friend in stunned amazement. You don't have a chance to respond because your friend continues, "There are a few more details about how our friendship is going to function. I know you might have times of need, sorrow, or joy, but I don't want to hear about it! This is a one-way street, and you are here to give to me. Got the picture?"

How would you feel? Is there any possibility that such a relationship would be healthy? What kind of hope would there be for any depth or mutual love? This kind of self-centered mind-set would destroy any friendship! As a matter of fact, the word friendship couldn't be used to describe such a relationship.

What if a husband or wife said to their spouse, "You exist for me! Serve me. Meet my needs. Make me happy. Feed me. Provide for me. Entertain me. You exist to do what I want. And by the way, I will not be doing anything for you. This relationship is all about me!"

There will never be health and wholeness in a relationship where this kind of attitude prevails. God's plan is for mutual love to be expressed in our relationships. When we become part of a local congregation, we are entering a living relationship with a family.

After all the time, prayer, and energy you have invested to find a church you can really love, now you have the privilege of giving back. Because the church is a body of people, it is a dynamic and growing relationship. Since the church is the bride of Christ, it is in a continual love affair with the Savior and his people.

Because the church is a family, loving and being loved will always be part of the equation.

Letting the Church's Purpose Become Your Purpose

As we have discovered, a biblical purpose is essential for a church to thrive. As members of Christ's church, we need to live out his purposes if we are going to flourish and grow. As we review the five purposes of the church, pray for an understanding of how you can grow in each area. The best way to love the church is to live in accordance with God's purposes for your life.

Going deeper as a worshiper. Showing up for a worship service and being a worshiper are two different things. Now that you have found a church home, commit to a lifetime of growing as a worshiper. Worship everywhere you go, in the workplace as you lift up silent prayers for those around you, in the car as you drive, in the crowded mall, on the sideline of a soccer game, and when you gather with God's people. You can worship wherever you are, but there is something powerful about gathering with the family of God to lift your heart in unison with the hearts of God's people.

Give your heart over to God in worship. Express your praise. Enter into prayer and let your spirit agree with the community of faith. Sing with passion. Humble yourself when the Word of God is preached, and invite the Holy Spirit to speak to you. Give with generosity. Greet other worshipers warmly. Come with an open heart, ready to meet with God. God deserves all of your praise. You are called to "love the LORD your God with all your heart and with all your soul and with all your strength" (Deut. 6:5). This is God's desire for you, and it should be a growing passion of your heart.

Be careful not to grow stagnant. Ask the Holy Spirit to blow like a mighty wind through your heart and mind to clear out any cobwebs. Pray for a fresh outpouring of the Holy Spirit every time you worship. Gather with God's people in expectancy, and when God shows up in a fresh and new way, celebrate his goodness. This kind of spirit will please God and will help you to grow as a worshiper.

Committing to ministry. In chapter 11, we warned against jumping into ministry responsibilities too quickly. Some people need a month or two before they are ready to begin serving; others need more time. We have met many people who enter the church with a severe case of burnout. It is wise for these people to hold back from serving for a season so that they can find refreshment for their souls and healing for their hearts. But ministry is part of God's call for everyone. If you are going to love your church, you need to discover your unique and God-given gifts, receive the necessary training to develop those gifts, and then serve with joy.

The role of pastors and teachers is to train, equip, and encourage all members of the church to do the work of ministry (Eph. 4:11–13). If you are not sure what specific gift or gifts God has given you to serve in the church, take a spiritual-gifts class at your church. If your church doesn't offer such a class, reading *Networking* by Bruce Bugbee will give you an introduction to spiritual gifts and will help you discover your God-given place in ministry.

When you know your spiritual gifting, find a place to serve others and glorify God. We suggest that you find only one or two areas of service and really invest yourself. It is better to do one thing well in the life of the church and find joy in it than to do four things poorly and become overextended and ineffective. Find an area of service and give yourself to it with passion and joy. Pray that God will use your hands, voice, mind, and all you are for his glory. There is so much joy when you feel the power of God fill you and the presence of the Holy Spirit flow through you as you serve God, his people, and the world!

Being passionate about evangelism. Jesus made it crystal clear that every one of his followers should be part of his plan to share God's love with the world. As a matter of fact, God's primary plan for reaching people who are not yet part of his family is us, his church, his people. Listen to what Jesus said about this:

> You are the salt of the earth. But if the salt loses its saltiness, how can it be made salty again? It is no longer good for anything, except to be thrown out and trampled by men.
>
> You are the light of the world. A city on a hill cannot be hidden. Neither do people light a lamp and put it under a bowl. Instead they put it on its stand, and it gives light to everyone in the house. In the same way, let your light shine before men, that they may see your good deeds and praise your Father in heaven.
>
> —Matthew 5:13–16

After Jesus died to pay the price for our sins and rose from the dead to show us the way back to the Father, he spoke these words:

> But you will receive power when the Holy Spirit comes on you; and you will be my witnesses in Jerusalem, and in all Judea and Samaria, and to the ends of the earth.
>
> —Acts 1:8

It is clear that Jesus was *not* making a casual suggestion. God calls every Christian to let their light shine. He wants our lives to have a saltiness that will cause others to thirst for the water of life that only he can give. We are all to go make disciples (followers) of Jesus. We are to do this right where we live (Jerusalem), in our extended community (Judea), even among our enemies (Samaria), and to the farthest reaches of the earth.

If you want to read a basic presentation of the message of salvation, we have provided one in the appendix of this book. If you have not yet made a personal commitment to enter a relationship with God through Jesus Christ, read the Gospel presentation in the back of this book and consider saying the prayer at the end. If you are not sure how to enter into God's evangelistic work, take a class on personal evangelism at your church or read the book *Becoming a Contagious Christian,* written by Mark Mittelberg, Lee Strobel, and Bill Hybels. Whatever you do, make sure you commit your life to telling others about how you entered a life-changing relationship with Jesus and what a difference it has made for you.

Building community. If you are going to love your church, you must learn to travel on a two-way street called community. You need to love people with God's love and allow them to love you back. Community is built as we serve others and invite them to minister to us in our times of joy and need. As the apostle Paul tells us, we need to care for each other in times of sorrow and celebration.

In a culture where we are taught to take care of ourselves, this teaching of Jesus is countercultural. It is radical. But it leads to fullness of life. We were born to be in community with God and with each other. We were created for intimacy. Just think about the biblical images we have written about in this book: we are a bride, a family, a body. We are connected!

Commit to building relationships with God's people. When you see people with needs, help meet them and care for those who are hurting. When you are struggling, don't keep it inside and go through times of pain alone. Let others minister to you. Get into a small group. Be on a service team. And whatever you do, always look for the new visitors and welcome them! Right now that feeling of walking into a church for the first time is still fresh in your heart. Over time you will forget what it felt like. But don't stop welcoming visitors and helping them see that your church is a loving community filled with the warmth and love of God.

Growing in discipleship. A church full of immature and self-seeking Christians is not a pretty sight. Discipleship is about growing up. It is about a commitment to maturity. One of the best ways you can love and strengthen your church is to be committed to growth. Spend time alone with Jesus each day and meet him as you pray, listen, read the Bible, and reflect deeply on his plan for your life.

Along with a commitment to personal spiritual growth, be ready to help others grow up in faith. No matter where you are in your spiritual journey, there are others you can help along the way. When you see an opportunity to encourage or gently challenge someone to grow in their love for God, do it! If you hear about an excellent book that will help you go deeper in your faith, read it and then pass it on to someone else. When your church offers a class or weekend seminar designed to help God's people grow in spiritual maturity, jump in!

As Christians, we are expected to continue in a lifelong pursuit of becoming more like Jesus. We are all called to grow up in our faith (Eph. 4:13–16). When we do, we give our church the best gift we can offer: ourselves, fully yielded to God.

Our Prayer for You

Being part of Christ's church is one of the greatest joys and privileges in all of life. Our prayer is that you will find a church you can really love. As we come to the end of this journey together, we join the apostle Paul in lifting up this prayer for you:

> For this reason, ever since I heard about your faith in the Lord Jesus and your love for all the saints, I have not stopped giving thanks for you, remembering you in my prayers. I keep asking that the God of our Lord Jesus Christ, the glorious Father, may give you the Spirit of wisdom and revelation, so that you may know him better. I pray also that the eyes of your heart may be enlightened in order that you may know the hope to which he has called you, the riches of his glorious inheritance in the saints, and his incomparably great power for us who believe. That power is like the working of his mighty strength, which he exerted in Christ when he raised him from the dead and seated him at his right hand in the heavenly realms, far above all rule and authority, power and dominion, and every title that can be given, not only in the present age but also in the one to come. And God placed all things under his feet and appointed him to be head over everything for the church, which is his body, the fullness of him who fills everything in every way.

—Ephesians 1:15–23

Appendix

The Apostles' Creed

I believe in God, the Father almighty,
creator of heaven and earth.

I believe in Jesus Christ, his only Son, our Lord,
who was conceived by the Holy Spirit
and born of the virgin Mary.
He suffered under Pontius Pilate,
was crucified, died, and was buried;
he descended to hell.
The third day he rose again from the dead.
He ascended to heaven
and is seated at the right hand of God the Father almighty,
from there he will come to judge the living and the dead.

I believe in the Holy Spirit,
the holy catholic church,★
the communion of saints,
the forgiveness of sins,
the resurrection of the body,
and the life everlasting. Amen.

★That is, the true Christian church of all times and all places.

The Nicene Creed

We believe in one God,
the Father almighty,
maker of heaven and earth,
of all things visible and invisible.

And in one Lord Jesus Christ,
the only Son of God,
begotten from the Father before all ages,
God from God,
Light from Light,
true God from true God,
begotten, not made;
Of the same essence as the Father.
Through him all things were made.
For us and for our salvation
he came down from heaven;
he became incarnate by the Holy Spirit and the virgin Mary,
and was made human.
He was crucified for us under Pontius Pilate;
He suffered and was buried.
The third day he rose again, according to the Scriptures.
He ascended to heaven
and is seated at the right hand of the Father.
He will come again with glory
to judge the living and the dead.
His kingdom will never end.

And we believe in the Holy Spirit,

the Lord, the giver of life.
He proceeds from the Father and the Son,
and with the Father and the Son is worshiped and glorified.
He spoke through the prophets.
We believe in one holy catholic and apostolic church.
We affirm one baptism for the forgiveness of sins.
We look forward to the resurrection of the dead,
and to life in the world to come. Amen.

The Best News Ever

There are many way to communicate the message of who Jesus is and what he did. In this brief appendix, we will present the Good News about Jesus (often called the Gospel) by walking through the core beliefs and biblical teaching about how a person comes to a saving relationship with God.

The Message of the Bible

God's love for people is huge and amazing

The Bible teaches, over and over again, that God loves us more than words can express. The whole story of the Bible is filled with God's love. The starting point of salvation is always God's love for us. No matter how we feel about ourselves and no matter how others might treat us, God's love is always constant! God longs to be in an intimate relationship with his people. He made us, loves us, and cares about us more than we could ever dream.

> But you, O Lord, are a compassionate and gracious God, slow to anger, abounding in love and faithfulness.
>
> —Psalm 86:15

> How great is the love the Father has lavished on us, that we should be called children of God! And that is what we are!
>
> —1 John 3:1

Human beings have broken their relationship with God by sinning

Sin is the word the Bible uses to describe anything we do that is not consistent with God's plan for us. Any thought that does not honor God, any word that is unkind, any action that hurts others or dishonors God is called sin. The Bible actually teaches that when we know there is something good that we should do and we fail to do it, this is also sin. In light of this, it becomes clear very quickly that we all sin quite a bit . . . every day.

Sin destroys our relationship with God. He still loves us, but our sin drives a wedge between us and him. God loves us and wants a restored relationship with us, but he can't just look the other way and pretend we have not sinned. Because God is perfectly pure (holy), he can't ignore sin. Because he is perfectly fair (just), he must punish sin. The Bible is clear that there is only one punishment for sin. It might sound harsh, but sin demands the death penalty. God's absolute holiness and unparalleled justice demand that this punishment be paid.

This is the worst news imaginable! Because of our sin, we are all separated from the God who loves us and condemned us to death because of our sin. This bad news can seem overwhelming, until we realize what God did so that we could be restored to relationship with him and be freed from the punishment and death sentence that hangs over us.

All have sinned and fall short of the glory of God.

—Romans 3:23

For the wages of sin is death, but the gift of God is eternal life in Christ Jesus our Lord.

—Romans 6:23

God did something about this problem,
and what he did is the greatest news ever

Thankfully, God's love is bigger than our sin. Our sin is real, and we are all under the condemnation of death. God's holiness keeps him from ignoring our sin, and his justice demands that the punishment be paid.

But God offers *to pay the price for us*. God came to this earth as a man, Jesus. This is what we celebrate at Christmas. Jesus was God in a human body. Jesus lived a real life, with real joys, pain, temptations, and he experienced everything we face. But here is the difference: Jesus never sinned. He did not have one thought, motive, or action that dishonored his Father. He never spoke a word that was hurtful or wrong. He never sinned!

Then, one day, he was accused of crimes he did not commit and was condemned to death. He was nailed to a cross and executed as a common criminal. He was stripped, beaten, mocked, and killed.

Jesus suffered this brutal death so that we would not have to pay the price for our sins. His death was the payment. We have sinned and deserve to die. Jesus sacrificed himself on the cross in our place. His death became ours. He did not deserve to die, but he did. We deserve to die, but we don't have to—if we accept Jesus and enter a relationship with God the Father through him.

The Gospel is called the Good News because we are offered a pardon for all the wrongs we have ever done, and ever will do. We can have new life and a restored relationship with God, through Jesus. We don't earn it or deserve it, and we can't take credit for it. All we can do is accept it.

For God so loved the world that he gave his one and only Son, that whoever believes in him shall not perish but have eternal life.

—John 3:16

This is love: not that we loved God, but that he loved us and sent his Son as an atoning sacrifice for our sins.

—1 John 4:10

How can a person accept Jesus, have their sins washed away, and enter a restored relationship with God?

The Bible is clear that salvation through Jesus is a free gift; it is not earned by checking the boxes on some to-do-list of good works. Salvation can be received only by faith in Jesus. This faith begins by praying and asking Jesus to be the one who forgives you and is the leader of your life. This step of faith means that you are admitting that you have sinned against God and that you are sorry for your sins. It means asking God to help you live a new and changed life that honors him.

You don't have to know a lot of fancy religious terms. Just tell God that you know you have sinned. Express your sorrow over your sin and ask for the forgiveness that comes through the price Jesus paid when he died on the cross. Then invite Jesus to enter your life and to lead you from this moment on, all the way into eternity. You can express this prayer in your own words, or you can use the following prayer:

Dear God, I am coming to you to express that I need you, that maybe I need you more than I have ever known. I want to admit that I have sinned. I have thought things, said things, and done things that do not please you. [At this point, you might want to be specific with God about some of the sins you are sorry about.] I realize that my sins cause me to be under a death sentence. I have also come to know that you sent Jesus, your only son, to pay the price for my sins by dying in my place. Jesus, I thank you for paying the price for me. I need your forgiveness, and I want you to enter my life and become my leader from this moment on. Thank you for all you have done and all you will do in my life, Amen!

When you have lifted up this prayer, you can be confident that you are now in a restored relationship with God and that all of your sins forgiven.

If we confess our sins, he is faithful and just and will forgive us our sins and purify us from all unrighteousness.

—1 John 1:9

As far as the east is from the west, so far has he removed our transgressions from us.

—Psalm 103:12

If you confess with your mouth, "Jesus is Lord," and believe in your heart that God raised him from the dead, you will be saved.

—Romans 10:9

A new beginning!

Making a commitment to follow Jesus and accepting his forgiveness is not the end of the road; it is the beginning of a whole new journey. A new life has started with Jesus at the center. If you are in the process of looking for a church and you have just prayed this prayer, we encourage you to share this fact with a leader of the church you are attending. Ask them what steps you should take to begin growing in your new faith.